The Devil Called
Collect

Books by J. Stephen Conn

Damascus Appointment (with Jerry Rutkin)
Run with the Vision (with Lester Sumrall)
Miracles Don't Just Happen (with Lester Sumrall)
Jesus Never Called Anyone a Sinner
Growing up Pentecostal
The Devil Called Collect

The Devil Called Collect

✦

The Exorcism of Jessica Leek

A True Story of Demonic Possession and Deliverance

J. Stephen Conn

iUniverse, Inc.
New York Lincoln Shanghai

The Devil Called Collect
The Exorcism of Jessica Leek

iUniverse books may be ordered through booksellers or by contacting:

iUniverse
2021 Pine Lake Road, Suite 100
Lincoln, NE 68512
www.iuniverse.com
1-800-Authors (1-800-288-4677)

Because of the dynamic nature of the Internet, any Web addresses or links contained in this book may have changed since publication and may no longer be valid.

ISBN: 978-0-595-47909-2 (pbk)
ISBN: 978-0-595-60166-0 (ebk)

Printed in the United States of America

All scripture quotations are taken from the authorized King James Version of the Bible, 1611.

To the memory of
Paul Dana Walker

And to Pastors
Randy and Mary Byrd

Dear friends and colleagues in ministry
Who have encouraged me to share this story

It is God alone who can cast out Satan. But he is generally pleased to do this by man, as an instrument in his hand; who is then said to cast out devils in his name, by his power and authority. And he sends whom he will send upon this great work; but usually such as man would never have thought of: For "his ways are not as our ways, neither his thoughts as our thoughts." Accordingly, he chooses the weak to confound the mighty; the foolish to confound the wise; for this plain reason, that he may secure the glory to himself; that "no flesh may glory in his sight."

John Wesley (1703–1791)
Founder of Methodism

Contents

Author's Preface

This is the true story of God's grace in the deliverance of a young woman from demonic possession. It began when Jessica Leek, a twenty-three-year-old practicing witch, called me long distance, collect in the middle of the night. As we talked, a guttural male demonic voice interrupted, speaking through Jessica's lips—blaspheming and threatening. Thus began one of the most incredible experiences I have had in a ministry which has spanned almost five decades.

Like all religions, Witchcraft comes in a wide variety of expressions. I was to learn that Jessica belonged to an order of the darkest kind, one that delved in black magic, consorted with demons, and even worshipped Satan.

After the very first telephone conversation with Jessica on that fateful March night in 1980, I immediately wrote it down verbatim, to the best of my ability, confirming my recollection of the call with my wife who had just listened in over the telephone extension. It was such an unusual experience that I didn't want to forget a single word.

Several calls followed. I kept a pen and notebook beside the telephone and took notes during each one. Immediately after hanging up the telephone, I wrote out each conversation exactly as it had transpired.

A few days later, I, along with an associate, Paul Dana Walker, met Jessica in person for the first time in a Savannah, Georgia, hotel. There we counseled and prayed with Jessica for several hours. It was an experience like none I had ever had. Numerous different demonic voices spoke through Jessica. At times the demons reacted violently when we prayed or read the scriptures. Although neither of us had ever been trained in exorcism, we used the authority of Jesus' name in an attempt to cast the demons out.

I had with me a pocket-sized tape recorder which I always carried during that period of my life. As a busy pastor, I used it to record notes, letters, etc. which were later transcribed by my secretary. With the recorder, I taped many of our conversations with Jessica, including the demonic voices. Much of the dialogue between me and the demonic entities which you will read in this book was taken verbatim from those tapes.

In order to continue ministering to Jessica, I took her to my home in Augusta, Georgia, where I lived with my wife and our three sons: Gregory, Christopher, and Jeromy. I would have hesitated to take her into my home if I had known what was to happen. On Jessica's second night with us, things became much more intense. She was not completely delivered until after an all-night exorcism which at times was violent and even life-threatening. A plethora of demonic entities manifested themselves through Jessica, speaking through her, identifying themselves by name, and manipulating their victim in uncanny ways.

Even though some of the things that were said by the demonic voices still puzzle me, I have not changed any of the wordings and have tried to present them in a way that does not favor any particular theological position. I simply share the events as they happened.

The very title of this book shows that it is a story which I did not seek; it came looking for me. I have often wondered why the Lord allowed me to have such an incredible experience. If God needed an exorcist, surely he knew that at best I was a very reluctant vessel—albeit a willing one. Perhaps it was because my heavenly father knew he could teach me to trust him more fully through the ordeal. While I have always been a believer, I have often been tempted to doubt.

The events recorded here were life changing for me. In the fifty-five years that I have been a born-again Christian, nothing has done more to confirm my faith. This story is presented to you, the reader, with the prayer that it will be a boost to your faith as well.

The manuscript has lain in the bottom drawer of a file cabinet in my study for more than twenty-seven years. It is presented here much as it was first written, except for the addition of a few minor updates, this preface, and an epilogue. I am indebted to my beautiful wife, Karen, for her expert editing and proofreading.

Those who have asked me why I waited so long to publish it deserve an honest answer.

First, there are elements of the story that did not correlate with my theological training. As a pastor who has spent a lifetime studying the Bible, there are some things about demons, possession, and deliverance that I still do not fully understand. I thought the day would come when I would have a more perfect knowledge. I would then present this story along with an in-depth teaching about exorcism.

Now that I am retired from the pastorate, I have accepted the reality that there are many things one will never fully comprehend on this side of eternity. *"For who hath known the mind of the Lord, or who hath been his counselor?"* Romans 11:34. Therefore, I present this story, exactly the way it happened, as a testimony and not as a thesis. Although this is not an instruction manual on casting out demons, there is still much that can be learned from the narrative. Readers may draw their own theological conclusions.

Secondly, I have hesitated to tell this story because I feared being branded as a kook. Even though the events recorded here are completely true, documented, and have been verified by credible witnesses, there are some who will not believe them. They will put this testimony in the same category as an alien abduction or a Bigfoot sighting. Others will offer a psychological explanation or dismiss the story as the product of an overactive imagination. However, I have no point to prove; I only have a testimony to share.

A third reason I did not publish the book earlier is because I did not want it to be seen as an advertisement of my services as an exorcist. When I shared part of this testimony with my own congregation, even as it was unfolding, news of the exorcism spread very quickly throughout the city and beyond. I was deluged with calls and visits from people who wanted me to cast demons out of them, their acquaintances, their homes and/or their pets. I did not refuse to counsel and pray with any of those who came to me. Most of them had very real prob-

lems—spiritual, emotional, mental or otherwise—but I considered few, if any of them, possessed. I've ministered to many
people over the years who were tempted, tormented, harassed,
and oppressed by the devil. But only once have I encountered
a person whom I was absolutely convinced to be possessed by
a legion of demons. That person was Jessica, the young
woman whose story you are about to read.

So after all these years, why publish the book now? Because
it is a story which needs to be told and in my spirit I feel the
time is right. Although I do not have all the answers—and
don't believe anyone does—the story has much value. Some
will be enlightened by it. Others will have confirmed to them
things they already know. Most of all, through this testimony,
some reader might find hope, encouragement, or faith.

Recently I have been reminded of a promise I made to the
Lord when I was sixteen years old. I shared that story in an
earlier book, *Growing up Pentecostal.* As a teenager, I felt
strongly that God was calling me to preach, but I wanted to be
sure it was God who was calling me and not just my own
desire. After months of sincere prayer, I decided to put the
decision in the Lord's hands. I promised him that, without my
telling anyone I wanted to be a minister, if I were ever invited
to preach, I would do it.

Shortly thereafter, I was asked to give a sermon to the
inmates at a county jail. After that first, faltering effort,
another invitation came, and then another—until soon I was
receiving more invitations to preach than I was able to accept.

I remembered that promise I had made to the Lord when I
was invited to come to two different churches and share this

remarkable testimony, twenty-seven years after it happened. The same pastors have also encouraged me to publish the story in a book, little knowing that I had written the manuscript so many years ago.

So here it is. Although the devil is a major character in this story, the hero is Jesus Christ. I trust that I have not glorified either myself or Satan. Rather, it has been my aim to give testimony to the power of the blood of Jesus and to the authority of the Bible, God's holy word.

J. Stephen Conn

Foreword

It has been twenty-seven years since I began following God's call in my life to pastor in the United Methodist Church. I started as a part time youth director in a downtown church in Augusta, Georgia. Paul Dana Walker, my best friend and College Age Ministry leader significantly encouraged me to take this first step. Most of my childhood and adolescent years were in Southern Baptist churches, so it probably is a bit surprising my credentials would include being involved in something as bizarre as demonic deliverance. I have been part of a great number of experiences in my years as a Christian and a pastor, but I can undoubtedly say this event was unlike any other. *I will quickly add that I have not had additional experiences nor have I felt a leading to take this us as a regular scheduled event in my weekly duties.*

The friendship with my pastor, Stephen Conn, and Paul Dana Walker opened an avenue for me to witness God's power of deliverance and love. I am not sure how God worked all the circumstances or "coincidences" in a way to include me, but I still remember that night in the Conn's family room as clearly as I did then. I can see the facial expressions, hear the voices and sounds, and stunningly remember the power of prayer as we witnessed demonic powers subjected to the name and the blood of Jesus. What I remember vividly was an absence of fear. Because of the genuine love for this young girl, who was tormented and trapped by evil, God's love cast out all fear.

As incredible as the story is, it never became a point of boasting in our mutual conversations. If anything, we shared with humility the honor to be used by God. Occasionally I have retold the happenings of this event to fellow brothers and sisters in Christ. As I share, I often find myself leaving out details because the story seems too incredible (it is not the usual illustration you hear from a United Methodist pastor in North Georgia). I am thankful that Stephen has recorded this memoir in such detail. *The Devil Called Collect* is a gift to today's Christian culture that often ignores, if not denies, the reality of demonic holds on people's lives. The greater story within the story is of a God, who through His ever loving, providential care, chooses to use willing servants to bring the hope of salvation in Jesus Christ to a lost soul.

In your reading, may you come to know the truths I experienced: there is no one so far removed from God that He cannot reach him or her; and God will answer whoever cries out and calls to Him, even when it is collect.

Grady Mosley

1

The Devil Called Collect

The jarring ring of the telephone awakened me from a deep sleep. Groggily, I picked up the receiver as I glanced at the clock. It was 2:00 AM.

Since I was the senior pastor of a large and growing congregation, I was accustomed to hearing the telephone ring at all hours. However, this was no everyday emergency call. The conversation which followed was one of the most bizarre I had ever experienced.

"I have a collect, long distance call for anyone from Jessica. Will you accept the charges?" the operator asked.

In my half awake mind, I could not think of anyone I knew by that name, but I reasoned that whoever it was must need help so I answered, "Yes, Operator, I will."

Next, I heard the pleading, soft, almost childlike voice of a young woman. "Hello, this is Jessica. Can you help me?"

"Where are you? What kind of help do you need?"

"I've been hitch-hiking and I'm on the side of the road in Atlanta. Somebody gave me your name and number and said that maybe you could help me."

"I would be very happy to do whatever I can to help you," I told her. "But, I'm in Augusta and that's 145 miles from Atlanta. Why don't you call the Mount Paran Church of God in Atlanta first thing in the morning? I believe their office opens at 8:30. There are lots of wonderful people there and they are close enough that maybe they could give you the help you need."

"But, I'm afraid," Jessica replied. "You see, I'm a witch of the fifth degree. I'm about to be initiated into the sixth degree of our Order and all of a sudden I'm scared. Strange things are going on and I'm afraid something bad might happen to me."

It wasn't my intention to put Jessica off or dismiss her lightly. She obviously needed help. But, I told her a second time, "I really think it would be better if you called the Mount Paran Church there in Atlanta." I let her know I was a personal friend with the pastor and some of his staff and I was certain they would do whatever they could to minister to her.

Jessica's voice became more pleading and desperate now. "But can't *you* help me?"

Witchcraft was definitely not a subject about which I knew a great deal. My experience in ministering to people trapped in the occult was limited. "Jessica," I answered, "to be truthful, I'm not sure whether I can help you or not. But I know someone who can. His name is Jesus Christ. Have you ever heard of Jesus? He has the answer you are looking for."

I was shocked when I was answered, not by Jessica, but by a man's curt, demanding voice. "No, no, you can't have her. Just hang up the phone. You can't have her. She is mine!"

I thought that Jessica must have had a boyfriend standing beside her in the phone booth who had been listening in on our conversation. "Who are you?" I asked.

What came next startled me as nothing ever had before. The guttural masculine voice spat back, "There are many of us."

For a split second, I thought "many of us" might refer to a group, like a motorcycle gang. Then, my mind flashed to the incident in the Bible where Jesus encountered the demon possessed maniac of the Gadarenes. When Jesus asked the man his name, the demons had answered through him, *"My name is Legion; for we are many."* Mark 5:9.

"How many are you?" I asked the voice.

"There are about three thousand of us here," came the demonic reply.

Now I was so wide awake that I knew I would not be able to sleep again that night. My wife was also awake, so I frantically motioned for her to get out of bed and go listen in on the kitchen telephone. She would be able to tell me that the voice I heard was real and not just a nightmare or a trick of my imagination at two o'clock in the morning.

I demanded of the voice, "If there are so many of you, then who are your leaders?"

In rapid succession, the voice spat out four names, "Orion, Adrian, Beelzebub, Leviathan."

I had heard of this kind of phenomenon but in nearly two decades of ministry, this was my first such personal encounter with demonic spirits. I had never made a particular study of how to deal with demons. Yet, a sudden resolve gripped me as I was now standing beside the bed. I was surprised to hear myself suddenly speaking with an authority that surpassed my normal demeanor. "Orion, Adrian, Beelzebub, Leviathan, I command you to go in the name of Jesus. I come against you and cast you out by the power of Jesus' blood. You must go and torment this girl no more."

The demons were not to be exorcised so easily. A wicked, mocking laugh came back. "No, we won't go. She is ours. You can't have her."

"No, Satan! Jessica has called me for help and I am a child of the most high God. She does not want you to be her lord any more. In the name of Jesus, I command you to go."

"No, we won't go."

"You have no choice. Be quiet and let me talk again to Jessica. Now go in Jesus' name."

I found myself listening once again to the pleading, soft voice of the young woman who had first called me. "What happened?" she asked in bewilderment. "Why are you talking to me like that? Are you mad at me? Where do you want me to go?"

"Oh, no, Jessica," I assured her. "I'm not angry with you at all. I was speaking to the demons that were talking through you. Did you not know that enemy spirits were using you to talk with me?"

"But there's no one here except me and the telephone and the radio."

"Jessica, do you know anyone by the name of Orion or Adrian?"

"Yes," she answered. "Those are some of the spirits that we use in our witchcraft. Why do you ask?"

"I was just talking to them through you, and also to Beelzebub and Leviathan. Were you not aware when they were talking through you?"

"That can't be," she insisted. "I know those spirits but they don't use me. I use them. They never appear unless I summon them to come."

"They have deceived you, Jessica," I explained. "You have allowed them to possess you and now you are no longer in control of the spirits but they have control of you."

I remembered the scripture, "*Hereby know ye that Spirit of God: Every spirit that confesseth that Jesus Christ is come in the flesh is of God: And every spirit that confesseth not that Jesus Christ is come in the flesh is not of God: and this is the spirit of antichrist....*" I John 4:2–3.

I had once heard an evangelist preach that a person who is truly demon possessed either can not or will not utter even the name of Jesus except in a blasphemous way. Although I felt that premise could not be proven unequivocally by scripture, I thought it might have some validity. I asked, "Jessica, have you ever heard of Jesus? Can you say Jesus?"

"Sure, I can say his name if I want to," she answered.

"Then say it, Jessica. Say Jesus."

"Jekkkk," came the reply, followed by a choking sound.

"Say Jesus, Jessica."

"Jekkkk."

"Jessica, can't you say his name? Can't you say Jesus?"

"But I said it," she replied in a puzzled voice.

"Jessica, you tried, but the enemy spirits hate Jesus, and they would not allow you to say his name," I told her. "Didn't you notice when they choked you off every time you tried to say 'Jesus?'"

"No, I thought I said it."

"Let's try this." I suggested. "Let me hear you say Jesus is Lord."

This time I heard the name of Jesus spoken clearly but it was not in Jessica's voice. A demon hissed defiantly, "Jesus is a pile of s__t."

"No!" I fired back. "Jesus is Lord! Jesus is Lord!"

"Jesus is a liar," came the demonic retort.

"Now, Devil," I demanded angrily. "I told you to go and I'm telling you again. Leave this girl and never come back to torment her any more."

"And who are you to tell me to go? You have no power over me."

A holy boldness welled up in me. "I am God's child. I am filled with his Holy Spirit and washed in Jesus' blood. It is not in my name but in his name that I say you must go."

"No, you can't make us go."

"Be quiet, Satan. I don't want to talk to you any more. I want to talk to Jessica. Now let me speak to her."

Once more the bewildered voice of a young woman spoke. "What happened? Where have you been? Did you leave the phone and go somewhere?"

I explained that I had been there all the time and the evil spirits had taken charge of her again and talked through her.

"Is that why I'm getting this terrible headache?" she asked.

"It might be, Jessica. I don't know for sure about that."

"Well, I'm getting thirsty too," she said. "Will you hold on for a while and let me go to get a drink?" I assured her I would wait.

For the next two minutes while Jessica was away from the telephone, I prayed fervently that God would direct me and somehow help me to reach this young woman who was so desperately in need of God's deliverance. Compassion as I have seldom experienced came over me and I felt almost a sense of desperation to reach out to this lonely, pleading voice and set her free in Jesus.

There was a rattle at the other end of the line and I heard Jessica say, "Okay, I'm back."

"Jessica, I'll do anything I can to help you," I volunteered. "Can you tell me where you are?"

"I'm in Atlanta."

"Atlanta is a very big place. Can you tell me exactly where you are in Atlanta?"

"I'm hitch-hiking and I don't know where I am for sure," she answered, "just somewhere."

"Listen to me very carefully," I instructed her. "I could never find you in a big city like that unless you tell me exactly where you are. As soon as you get to any place that you can tell me where to find you, then please call me back. Wherever you are, I will come and get you. If you don't want me to come for you, then please come to Augusta and meet me here. Do you understand me?"

"I understand you," she puzzled, "but why do you want me to come to Augusta?"

"Remember, you called me and asked if I could help you. Well, I can and I want to. But, I can't do it over the telephone. We need to get together."

"No!" I was interrupted again by the mocking voice of a demon. "We will not let her come. We will kill her first. We will not allow her to meet you."

I rebuked Satan once more and forbade him to hinder Jessica from reaching me. In the name of Jesus, I bound any power he had to harm her. Then, I spoke a final word to Jessica.

"Whatever you do," I urged, "don't lose my telephone number. Hold on to it as if your life depended on it because it's my only link with you. Please, please call me back as soon as you know where you are. I'll be praying that you will make it to Augusta."

"Okay," she said. "I'll call you." A click signaled she had hung up the receiver.

I slowly returned my telephone to the night stand. The moment the telephone hit the cradle, it was ringing again—now at 2:30 AM.

"Hi, Stephen, this is Don." I recognized the voice as that of Donald Goodrum, a friend I had known since our college days together. Don was now pastor of a church in west Tennessee. I had not seen him for several years.

"Have you been talking with Jessica Leek?" Don asked.

"I didn't know her last name was Leek, but yes, I have been talking with Jessica. How did you know?"

Don told me the same young woman had called him first and he had referred her to me since I was the only minister he could think of off hand in the state of Georgia. He said someone had given her a gospel tract with his name and telephone number on it. At least that explained the mystery of how Jessica had gotten my number.

After I hung up from talking with Don, I laid back down on the bed and stared at the ceiling almost in disbelief. I asked my wife, Pat, "Did you hear what I just heard? Was that real?"

"I heard it," Pat said, "but I never heard anything like it."

After a few minutes of stunned silence, I mused, "Can you believe I've been actually talking to the devil? And, he didn't even pay for the call. The devil called collect."

I stayed in bed but did not go back to sleep until after the sun came up a few hours later. As I awaited the sunrise, I prayed silently, but fervently, that God would somehow help Jessica reach me, or help me reach her, the following day.

2

The Light Went Out

o o o o o o o o o o o o o o o o o o o o o o o o o o o

Wherefore we would have come unto you, even I Paul, once and again; but Satan hindered us.

—1 Thessalonians 2:18

Pray often; for prayer is a shield to the soul, a sacrifice to God, and a scourge for Satan.

—John Bunyan (1628–1688)
English Minister and Author

The next morning, Wednesday, dawned as dreary as my spirits. A heavy, cold rain fell throughout the day.

Out of a sense of duty, I went to the church office for a couple of hours since Wednesday morning was the set time I held a weekly staff meeting. I told the other ministers of our pastoral team of my strange telephone conversation with Jessica and the demon voices the night before. I asked them to pray with me that God would help us to somehow reach this troubled young woman and see her delivered. At the time, I was not absolutely certain the telephone call and the voices I had heard had not been just an elaborate hoax. If it was real, I wasn't sure whether Jessica was mentally ill or demon possessed—or both.

I was very tired from having gotten so little sleep the night before. Even more, I felt an unusual urgency to reach Jessica and try to help her. I returned home from the office around noon so I would be available if she called again. I left the house only once that afternoon, for less than an hour, to keep an appointment. During that brief time, Jessica called. She left a message that she was somewhere on the side of the road; she wasn't sure exactly where. She said she was trying her best to get to Augusta and would call again later.

I fervently prayed throughout the day that Jessica would not lose my number, that God would send his guardian angels to watch over her, and that she would call me. As I was praying, I remembered how just a week earlier I had completed a four day fast, drinking water but taking no food.

When I had fasted in the past, it was usually because I was burdened with some particular problem or was seeking God's guidance or help concerning a difficult situation. This time it had been different. There were no particular problems either in my personal life or in our congregation at the time—quite the contrary—things were going great. Ever since I had planted the church, a little more than three years earlier, we had enjoyed remarkable success. Attendance had grown from zero to a high of more than seven hundred. Both *Moody Monthly* and *Christian Life* magazines had named us the "Fastest growing church in Georgia." The editor of the *Augusta Chronicle* had called me "the best known pastor in Augusta," out of a metropolitan area with more than 400 local churches. Yet, in spite of our achievements, I longed to see more than just numeric growth and the accolades of people. I had a deep spiritual hunger to experience the supernatural hand of God at work.

As I had prayed during that fast, I had not asked for anything in particular—only that God would reveal himself to me and let me know his reality. I had prayed, "Here I am Lord, reporting for duty. Please show yourself to me and use me any way you will."

Perhaps—just perhaps—I thought, God had been preparing me for this assignment and was answering my prayer in a way I never would have imagined. The words of Jesus came to my mind as he had once spoken after casting demons out of a tormented soul, *"Howbeit this kind goeth not out but by prayer and fasting."* Matthew 17:21.

At the same time, I felt I was a very unlikely vessel for God to use in casting out devils. I had very little training or experience in the arena of spiritual warfare. Also, I felt that for a man of faith, I had more than my share of doubts. Although I was a true believer, over the years I had often prayed as did the desperate father who once brought his demon possessed son to Jesus: *"Lord, I believe; help thou mine unbelief."* Mark 9:24

It was not until 10:30 on Wednesday evening that the telephone rang and I heard the welcomed voice of the operator saying, "I have a collect call for anyone from Jessica. Will you accept the charges?"

I told the operator I would and was soon greeted by Jessica's soft, haunting voice. "Where are you, Jessica?" I asked.

"I'm in Savannah."

Savannah is about the same distance from Augusta as Atlanta, but in the opposite direction. Jessica explained that she had hitched a ride with a trucker, had fallen asleep, and had traveled all the way to Savannah before waking. I offered to come to Savannah immediately if she would only give me an address or directions to where she was staying. Jessica refused, saying she was staying with the man who had given her the ride and he would not let her tell where he lived for fear of getting into trouble.

As on the night before, I carefully instructed Jessica to keep my number, to try to come to Augusta, and to call me again as soon as she could tell me where she was.

Then she asked disarmingly, "Who are you anyway?"

"My name is Stephen, Jessica. Don't you remember talking to me from Atlanta last night?"

"I don't remember anything from last night," she said. "I was stoned. But I'm sober now. All I know is that I've got this number here and something keeps telling me that I've got to come to Augusta and I have to call you."

I assured Jessica that the something which told her those things was right. By all means, she must not stop trying until she had reached me.

"But, what for?" she inquired. "I don't even know you."

"You called me for help, Jessica. And I want to help you."

"How come? I don't need any help. I'm doing just fine. I think maybe we had better just forget this whole thing."

"Jessica," I insisted, "I can help you find the love, the joy, and the peace that Jesus Christ gives."

"Love? Peace? Joy? I already have those things," she said. "When I drop acid, I have joy; when I smoke pot, I have peace; when I go to bed with a man, I have love. I already have all that so what do I need you for?"

Suddenly, the voice to which I was speaking changed from that of a sweet, young girl to that of a snarling, older woman who began to curse and rave. I asked the voice, "Who are you?"

"I'm Jessica," the voice spat back.

"Oh no, you are not Jessica. I was talking to Jessica a moment ago. Who are you?" I was surprised at my own confidence and I felt a strong assurance that God was guiding my thoughts and words.

"I am Jessica," the voice insisted in a gruff, angry tone.

"In the name of Jesus, tell me your name!"

"Diana."

"And in whose name do you speak? By what power?"

"I speak in my own name," the demonic voice taunted.

"No." I rebuked, "I want to know in whose name you speak."

"I speak in the name of Satan and by the power of Hell," came the reply. "In whose name do you speak?"

"Diana," I said, "I come against you in the name of Jesus Christ and I command you by the power of His blood to loose this girl and let her go."

Jessica's voice returned and I asked her, "Do you know a Diana?"

"Yes," she said, "we have a goddess Diana. I go to the Church of Nature and she is a goddess that we worship."

I asked "Did you know that Diana was just speaking to me through you?"

"Well, I don't know about that but I know I am a medium and sometimes in séances the dead speak through me, but never Diana." She went on to explain that the dead could speak through her as a medium only at certain times in the afternoon when conjured up and she was always aware when it happened. She repeated what she had told me the previous evening—that the spirits did not use her but she used them. I reiterated to Jessica that the spirits had lied to her and deceived her. I told her she thought she possessed supernatural power, but in reality the supernatural beings possessed her. These spirits, I explained, were evil and would destroy her if she did not get rid of them.

"How do you know these things?" she asked.

"Because I have a supernatural gift that tells me."

Her voice registered surprise. "Are you into witchcraft?"

'I'm into spiritual things," I answered truthfully.

"What is your gift?"

I told her, "It is one of the gifts of the Holy Spirit and is called the gift of discerning of spirits."

Jessica's interest was really aroused now and the questions came fast. "Well, how did you get this gift? Do you have rituals that you go through?"

I silently prayed for divine wisdom to answer and said, "You might call them rituals. We have prayers that we pray."

"Do you have sacrifices? What about blood sacrifices?"

"Oh, yes, Jessica, yes. It's the greatest sacrifice that has ever been made. We have the sacrifice of the blood of God's own Son, Jesus. Haven't you heard of his blood?"

I proceeded to explain to her that the supernatural power I could share with her was far greater than any power she had ever known. I told her it was a power of love, mercy, kindness, and goodness.

I asked again, "Jessica, do you know Adrian, Orion, Leviathan, Beelzebub and Diana?"

"Yes, I know all of them."

"Jessica, they all have supernatural power, but this power I am telling you about is far greater than all of theirs put together. I want to share this power with you."

She asked, "But, how can I trust you?"

"And how can I trust you?" I countered. "Jessica, you have called me for help and that thing which is making you keep calling me back is a spirit. He is the Holy Spirit. It is the Holy Spirit's power, far greater than yours, that is drawing you to me. Do you understand?"

A sinister man's voice replied, "Yes, I understand. Now why don't you just hang up the phone?"

"To whom am I speaking now?" I asked.

"Moloch."

"Moloch, you be quiet. I'm talking to Jessica. I cast you out in the name of Jesus."

"No you don't," was the defiant reply.

More strongly than before, I responded to Moloch, "I come against you by the power of Jesus' blood and I say that you are damned to Hell."

I expected to hear Jessica's voice again but this demon seemed to be more tenacious than the ones I had dealt with previously. "I'm still here," was his mocking reply.

"But you are on your way out." I said to Moloch. "You cannot stand against the name of Jesus."

"You have no power against me," the voice taunted. "I'm still here. See, you cannot make me go. Why don't you just hang up? You're not going to be able to pay the bill if you keep talking on the phone."

"It is not in my name and not in my power," I persisted. "In the name of Jesus and by the power of His blood that was shed at Calvary, you must go."

Jessica's bewildered voice returned, "What! What happened?"

I explained I had been talking through her to Moloch. She told me she knew of Moloch. "He is a brother with Satan."

I repeated my instructions that Jessica must not allow anything to prevent her from getting to me. When she hung up the phone, it was with the promise she would try to come to Augusta the next day and that she would call me back.

Thursday was an even more trying day than Wednesday had been. Again, I spent most of the day at home near the telephone, afraid that I might miss Jessica's call if I was away. A smorgasbord of doubts paraded through my mind. As surreal as the telephone calls had been, I was certain that I had actually received the calls because, at my request, my wife had always been on the line to confirm and help me remember the bizarre conversations. In fact, I had taken notes during the telephone conversations and had tried to write them down verbatim as soon as they were over. This was such an unusual experience that I didn't want to forget a single detail. Surely my mind wasn't just playing tricks on me.

If this is just an unusually clever and persistent hoaxer, I reasoned, then how would she have known Donald Goodrum, my pastor friend from Tennessee who had called me that first night? Why did I have such an overpowering compassion in my heart for this stranger on the telephone unless it was from God? Still, I wondered if the whole thing might not just be someone's warped idea of a practical joke. Yet, the thought of a possessed young woman being somewhere on the side of the road trying to reach me besieged and dominated my thoughts.

Whatever the case, I spent the entire day praying. "God, please help me find her. Please protect her. Please let her call me again." At half past midnight, she did.

"Where are you, Jessica?"

"I'm in Aiken," she said.

"Aiken! Praise the Lord. That's just twenty miles from Augusta. Where are you in Aiken?"

Jessica said all she knew was that she was in a phone booth in front of a bar which was closed. Aiken is not a large city, but it was big enough to have a few dozen phone booths along the side of the road, so I questioned her very closely, asking her to describe the place to me in detail. I learned she was on the side of a long hill; a used car lot was across the street; there were no traffic lights in sight but there were street lights; it was a four lane highway and she could see a sign far up the road on which she read the word "Aiken."

I insisted Jessica not move from that spot for any reason. I would come and find her. I instructed her that it might take me an hour or more but I would hurry as fast as I could and that she was to wait. She could not give me the number of the telephone from which she was calling because she said it was blurry.

As I hurriedly dressed, I called the youth minister of our church, Paul Dana Walker. He said he would be ready in ten minutes, which is about the time it took me to reach his apartment. Paul Dana was waiting when I pulled up to his front door. I brought him up to date on the happenings of the past two days as we crossed the Savannah River into Aiken County, South Carolina.

Both of us were excited. We expected a long and fruitful night. Instead, the night was long and futile.

Even though it was well past midnight as we left for Aiken, my wife called two couples from our church whom she knew to be men and women of prayer. They called others and by the time the sun rose the following morning, there must have been 100 people praying for us. By the end of the next day, there would be several times that many praying as word spread. It surprised me that the entire congregation took such an intense interest in a troubled young woman of whom they had just heard and knew very little.

I normally would not have called people for prayer at such a late hour of the night. However, I was very pleased to learn that those who were called considered it a privilege to be able to lend prayer support to our spiritual warfare.

It took Paul Dana and me an hour and a half to find the telephone booth which fit Jessica's description. It was on a long hill on a four lane highway and across from a used car lot. There were street lights but no traffic signals visible, a sign up the road said "Aiken", and even the number on the telephone was smudged and illegible. Every detail was exactly as Jessica had given us except that it was in front of a closed liquor store instead of a bar. The defunct store did have a couple of liquor signs outside just in front of the telephone booth.

But, there was no Jessica. A cruising police car stopped momentarily along the side of the road in front of the store as we were looking around. Paul Dana and I got back into our car and the police car drove on.

It was almost three o'clock in the morning when we reluctantly went to the city police station ourselves. This was a last resort. We thought that perhaps Jessica had been picked up for vagrancy or on drug charges. The police told us no young women had been booked or reported that evening.

Weary and discouraged, Paul Dana and I started back toward Augusta. Driving once again past the telephone booth from which we thought Jessica had called, we noticed a house next door with the living room light burning, at three o'clock in the morning. In front of the house was the sign of a palm reader. As we drove past, the light went out.

3

A Holy Urgency

○ ○

When the even was come, they brought unto him many that were possessed with devils: and he cast out the spirits with his word, and healed all that were sick:

—Matthew 8:16

To discern spirits we must dwell with Him who is holy, and He will give the revelation and unveil the mask of Satanic power on all lines.

—Smith Wigglesworth (1859–1947)
Pioneer Pentecostal Minister

I woke up tired Friday morning. What little sleep I had gotten the night before had been troubled after our futile search for Jessica in Aiken. A very long day faced me.

In the morning, there were many telephone calls from church members wanting to know the results of the previous night's trip to South Carolina and also assuring me of their prayers. I appreciated the interest of my parishioners, but frankly, I was in no particular mood to talk about it. I felt discouraged—defeated.

Who were these voices on the telephone anyway? Why was I so obsessed with the thought of getting to Jessica? Why had I failed thus far? And if this was an assignment from God, why had he given it to me and not someone who would have relished the opportunity more?

My aspiration as a minister was to encourage people, not to cast demons out of them. I was pleased that I was beginning to develop a reputation not only as a preacher but also a motivational speaker. I was called on occasionally to address civic clubs, business groups, schools, and even the United States Army. In those settings, I was often introduced as a newspaper columnist or an inspirational speaker. I liked that. The last thing I wanted to be known as was an exorcist.

That day I sat in my study at home for several hours. I tried to pray but it didn't amount to much. The devil seemed to be having a field day with my mind. If God was real and if He had called me to be his minister, I reasoned, then where was His power? Was God bound by space? Why couldn't Jessica have been completely delivered when I rebuked the demons in His name over the telephone the first night she called? And, why couldn't I get to her?

To me, this was a clear cut struggle between the power of God and the power of Satan. So far, it seemed the devil was winning. I could imagine him laughing at us as Paul Dana and I had searched the streets of Aiken unsuccessfully the night before. The demons had said they would not allow Jessica to come to me and apparently, they were right.

I seriously questioned whether or not I should continue to be a minister. I pondered, here I have been preaching for all of these years and this is the first time I've had such an overt encounter with the devil. If whatever power I have with God is useless against demons, then I might as well quit calling myself a preacher. I thought much about how I would go about resigning my church and what I would do for a living.

With everything in me, I prayed and hoped Jessica would call back. But, I was tempted to believe the enemy when he whispered to my mind that I would never hear from her again.

At 2:45 PM, the phone rang and proved my worries to be unnecessary. It was another collect call from Jessica. I could have shouted. In fact, I did. This time she was in a rather jovial mood and talked for a while like a school girl who was just passing the time of day.

Jessica informed me she was back in Savannah and was staying with some friends. Something just wouldn't let her come to Augusta, or let her tell me how to find her. When I asked her for an address or telephone number, she said she was not allowed to tell me but that it was down the street from the Greyhound bus terminal. I then volunteered to wire a ticket to Jessica so she could come to Augusta.

"But why do you want me to come?" she asked.

"Because I want to help you."

"Why?"

"Because I love you," I blurted.

"Yeah," she laughed. "I bet you love me. A lot of men love me."

I quickly explained that I was not talking about an erotic or sensual love but a Godly love. I told her it was a spirit—the spirit of God—that loved her through me.

"You mean you have a spirit in you?" she inquired. "Where did you get this spirit?" Then she volunteered, "I was born with spirits in me."

"Well, I received my spirit by being born a second time," I told her.

"You mean like being reincarnated?"

I explained it was something better than reincarnation. I had been adopted into God's family, becoming his child, and that was called being born again.

Jessica expressed fear about my suggestion of sending her a bus ticket. "How do I know you won't get me up there and hold me against my will?"

That was a good question. She didn't know. I was sure my credentials as an ordained Christian minister would not impress her favorably. She was from a world which mistrusted all Christians and looked upon Jesus himself as the personification of evil.

I offered a round trip ticket. She said that sounded good, but she would have to wait for three days because this was an unlucky time for her to travel. Then she sighed, "Oh, why don't we just forget the whole thing. I'm getting tired of playing this game. I don't know what I called you for in the first place so why don't I just hang up this phone and get out of your life. Okay?"

A holy urgency came over me. If what she had told me earlier was true, by the end of three more days, Jessica would have been inducted into the sixth degree of her particular order of witchcraft. It was her apprehension about that which had prompted her to call me in the first place.

I began to order her firmly, "Jessica, in Jesus' name you will come to me. You will allow me to help you. You will not be held back by any evil spirit."

I was interrupted by a sinister demon that identified himself as Mephistopheles. I asked Mephistopheles where he came from and he said he was a fallen angel. I ordered him to be quiet and forbade him to prevent me from speaking to Jessica.

When Jessica's puzzled voice spoke again, I asked her if she knew of a spirit by the name of Mephistopheles. She told me she did not know this spirit personally but she had heard other witches speak of him. "He is the spirit who negotiates for the souls of people," she said. "He is the one I will deal with in a few days at my induction into the sixth degree."

She continued to tell me that Mephistopheles was the demon which had done the negotiations with many of the rock stars who sold their souls to the devil in return for fame and riches.

I informed Jessica that Mephistopheles was an evil spirit who could not be trusted and desired to destroy her soul. That was the reason she must come to me. I could help her find this power that was greater than any she had ever known before.

"What you're saying to me is beginning to make sense," Jessica pondered. "If you are really telling me the truth, I think I want this Holy Spirit you are talking about."

"Then, may I send you a bus ticket?" I asked.

"I'm still afraid," she answered. "Something inside keeps telling me I can't trust you. If you really want to see me as bad as you say you do, then why don't you come to Savannah?"

"But you won't give me an address."

"No," she said, "I can't. Just come to Savannah and I will find you."

We made arrangements for me to check in at a certain hotel and I assured her I would be there by seven o'clock that very evening. Jessica promised to call me at the hotel at eight. It was already three o'clock and Savannah was almost a three hour drive away.

I began to impress upon Jessica how important it was for her to get in touch with me since I would have no way of finding her in Savannah. She said, "Don't worry. I promised, and I cannot break a promise or I will lose my being and will become as nothing." One of the rules of witchcraft, she told me, was that she must tell the truth at all times. That statement within itself was a lie.

Our conversation was interrupted by the most heinous sounding voice I had yet heard. This demon, who identified himself as Ariel, spoke vehemently, "Do not come! If you come, I will take care of you when you get here."

I informed Ariel that I was coming to Savannah and in Jesus' name I bound his power to stop me. I also forbade him from doing anything to Jessica. I then commanded him to be gone.

Jessica's voice returned; I asked if she knew Ariel. "Yes, he is the spirit that casts evil spells upon people," she said.

Immediately after hanging up the phone with Jessica, I called the hotel in Savannah and made a reservation. The clerk told me it was the last room he had available that night. I called Paul Dana, my youth minister, and told him to cancel all plans for the evening. We had an appointment with the devil.

My wife had been listening in on the other telephone at my suggestion. She came into the room where I was and quietly asked, "Did you hear Ariel? He said he was going to take care of you when you got to Savannah. Are you still going?"

I said, "Pat, I've never wanted to do anything in my life any more than I want to see God deliver that girl. You couldn't stop me for anything on earth. If the Bible I have been preaching for all these years is not true, if God's power is not greater than that of the devil, the last twenty years of my life have been wasted. If that's the case, I had just as soon die now and take my chances on what lies beyond. But if the power of God is all that I believe it to be, we have nothing to fear."

In thirty minutes, Paul Dana and I were on the road to Savannah.

4

On The Devil's Turf

○ ○

For we wrestle not against flesh and blood, but against principalities, against powers, against the rulers of the darkness of this world, against spiritual wickedness in high places.

—Ephesians 6:12

It is no marvel that the devil does not love field preaching! Neither do I; I love a commodious room, a soft cushion, a handsome pulpit. But where is my zeal if I do not trample all these underfoot in order to save one soul?

—John Wesley (1703–1791)
Founder of Methodism

It was about seven o'clock and the sun was just setting that Friday evening when Paul Dana and I saw the highway signs welcoming us to Savannah. The words of the demon Ariel kept running through my mind. "If you come, I will take care of you when you get here." As we entered the city limits, I shuddered. We were now on the devil's turf.

Jessica did not call at eight o'clock as she had promised. Paul Dana and I prayed a little, read our Bibles a little, and stared at the telephone. I switched on the television for a couple of minutes but neither of us was in the mood to watch, so I turned it back off. We waited in silence, but both of us were silently praying.

We were not the only ones keeping vigil. When Paul Dana and I had left for Savannah, his wife, Julie, called my wife, and then Julie called the members of the college/career sharing group from our church and asked them to meet at our house for a time of special prayer. Another prayer group within the church heard what was happening and also called an emergency prayer meeting. Others in our congregation got together with friends in their homes to hold us up in prayer. I later learned that some from the college/career group did not go home the entire night but continued in prayer until daylight the next morning when my wife served them breakfast.

The telephone in our hotel room rang at midnight. It was Jessica. She said she had gone to a party out on the beach, twenty-seven miles from town, and she couldn't get back to Savannah until the next morning.

I did not know whether Jessica was telling me the truth or was merely playing some diabolical game. I informed her we could wait only until check-out time at 11:00 AM and then we would have to leave. I needed to be back in Augusta for weekend church services.

Jessica began to cry. I had never heard her cry before. "Please don't leave before I get to see you," she pleaded. "If what you have been telling me is the truth, then I think I want this power you have."

Jessica called again at 7:30 the next morning to say she was on her way to our hotel in a taxi. I agreed to meet her at the front door and pay the fare.

Jessica was a rather ordinary looking girl, medium height, heavy set, long straight dark hair, and a pretty face. She wore blue jeans, sandals, and a loose fitting blouse. What I noticed most were her rings—four on one hand and three on the other. All were silver and all had designs representing the occult. On one wrist was a silver bracelet decorated with two silver ram's heads.

"Do you mind if we have breakfast first?" she asked. "I'm starved."

I glanced at Paul Dana and back to Jessica. "Would you like to have something sent to the room?" I suggested.

"Don't worry," Jessica laughed. "I'm not dangerous. We can eat in the restaurant."

Paul Dana and I weren't sure we believed her, but we ordered a table for three. Our conversation at breakfast was cordial but guarded. We dared not talk of Jesus Christ or spiritual things for fear that the demons might manifest themselves in public. It would have been hard to explain.

Once we were back in the hotel room, I began to recount with Jessica the events of the past four days. Her memory of them was vague, and most parts she said she didn't remember at all. She didn't seem to know exactly why or how the three of us had come to be in the hotel room on this cool March morning.

As we began to talk about Jesus, the conversation became extremely frustrating. Jessica would repeatedly lapse into a trance. Her eyes took on a blank, glassy stare and she would sit motionless and without expression. Sometimes she would only remain in the trancelike state for a few seconds and then snap back with a start saying, "What? What did you say? I'm sorry, but I didn't hear what you were saying."

At other times, the trances lasted longer and Paul Dana and I would pray, rebuking the spirits that bound her thoughts and stole the word of God from her mind.

Finally, we were able to have this conversation.

"Jessica, what do you think about Jesus?"

"I don't know. Why?"

"Do you know who Jesus is?"

"Well, my mom said he was a man who lived a long, long time ago. I mean a *long* time ago. And, he went around begging money from people, getting into people's heads, and things like that. She called him a psychic man, one who did spiritual healings. He became a martyr at the end. When he was dead, he was dead, and that was the end of it."

"Didn't they tell you Jesus rose from the dead?" I asked.

"No."

"He did!" I said.

"Well, good for him."

"They didn't tell you he was the Son of God?" I asked.

"No."

"He is!"

"That's nice," she replied flippantly.

"They didn't tell you that Jesus not only lived long ago, but he is still alive today?"

"No!" she said, now visibly irritated.

"Jessica," I continued, "that's what Paul Dana and I want to share with you. There is a God who is good. There is a spirit and a power personified in Jesus Christ, the Son of God, who is far greater than any power or spirit you have ever known."

At this point, she lapsed into another one of her trances. Paul Dana and I prayed, commanding her to come back in Jesus' name.

After Jessica regained her senses, we asked if she was aware of the lapses of consciousness which she was experiencing. She told us that normally it only happened at certain times of the day when she allowed the spirits to take charge. She expressed bewilderment and concern that she no longer seemed to have any control over her own mind.

I explained that she was possessed of spirits which were evil and would eventually destroy her if she was not delivered of them.

Jessica began to question me. "Are you sure you're not some kind of a witch?" She said she could tell I knew a lot about the spirit realm and there was something about my eyes that she could not quite understand. I explained, as I had told her on the telephone earlier, that I *was* into spiritual things. However, the spiritual realm I dealt in was on the positive side while witchcraft was negative.

She then commented on my aura. According to Jessica, it was all shiny yellow and blue, signifying a state of perfect balance and peace. Hers was usually brown and green, she said.

I let her know that if my aura was brighter than hers, it was because of no merit of my own. I was no better and of no greater value than she. It was simply that I had received a gift from God—one which she could also receive if she willed to do so.

I brought the conversation back to the subject of Jesus and immediately Jessica lapsed into another trance. Paul Dana and I commanded the malevolent spirits to loose her. Several times she would return but as soon as we mentioned the name of Jesus again, she would fall back into a stupor. It was extremely frustrating.

Very slowly, I shared with Jessica the simple story of the Gospel. I told her there is only one true and living God and he loved her very much. This God had a son whose name is Jesus. Jesus loved her so much he made the greatest blood sacrifice ever known by giving his life for her.

Not knowing whether or not Jessica understood the things I had just shared, I began to question her. "Who was God's Son?"

Her only answer was a blank stare.

"Tell me, Jessica, what is the name of God's Son?"

Jessica's eyes rolled wildly, almost as if she were choking, and she belched, "Jekkkk."

"And who made the greatest blood sacrifice ever known?"

"Was it Levi?" she asked. Levi, Jessica said, was the name of one of her grandfathers.

Paul Dana, who had been praying silently, jumped into the conversation, "No, it was not Levi. It was Jesus, the Son of God. He died for you."

"Well, let's not get angry about it," Jessica laughed.

"I'm just telling you that Jesus died for you," Paul Dana said.

"For me? For me?" she retorted in a sarcastic, high pitched tone.

"Yes," Paul Dana said emphatically, "Jesus died for you."

"Wheeeee," Jessica squealed, throwing her hands into the air.

"And do you know why he died for you?" Paul Dana continued, "Because he loves you."

"NO!" It was a growling male demon's voice which answered this time. Not only did Jessica's voice change, but also her expression—dramatically so. An indescribable satanic countenance fell across her face. The most frightening thing was the look in her eyes—as if some creature other than Jessica was peering out at us.

I had heard the demon voices over the telephone but this was the first time I had witnessed Jessica's expression as they spoke through her. It was unnerving. A chill seemed to fill the room and the hairs on my arms stood at attention.

Paul Dana rebuked the demon, telling him that he was a defeated foe. The demon protested and refused to leave but Paul Dana spoke again with authority and Jessica returned to her senses. She slumped deflated into her chair with the cowering, pleading expression of a frightened little child.

"Jessica," I said. "I believe you would like to know Jesus. I believe you would like to know the God who is above all gods, the Lord above all lords, and the Spirit that is far greater than any other spirit—the Creator Spirit of the world."

"Is he the creator of earth?"

"Yes."

"Air?"

"Yes."

"Fire?"

"Yes."

"Water?"

"Yes, Jessica. He created all these things. He is the Creator of the whole world. Wouldn't you like to know him?"

"I wouldn't be here if I didn't want to talk about it," she replied.

"Jessica," I instructed, "If you want to know Jesus, all you've got to do is invite him into your heart."

"You've got to be kidding," she responded. "No candles? No rituals?"

I explained to her that she could just talk to God in the same way she was talking to me and Paul Dana. I asked if she would allow us to pray with her right then.

Jessica replied by pointing across the room and saying, "If you will do it from way over there."

As she was speaking, her voice and personality abruptly changed. A demon taunted sarcastically through her lips. "You just go ahead and pray. I dare you to pray. I have no need to pray."

We took the devil's dare and also honored Jessica's request. Standing on the far side of the room from Jessica, Paul Dana and I began praying that she would see her need of the Saviour. Our prayers were interrupted by a sinister voice from her lips which ordered, "Leave this girl alone."

It seemed that we were making no progress and I felt a sense of frustration, not really knowing how to pray under the circumstances. The scripture flashed into my mind *"… for we know not what we should pray for as we ought, but the Spirit itself maketh intercession for us with groanings which cannot be uttered … according to the will of God."* Romans 8:36–37. I began to intercede for Jessica in another tongue—my prayer language.

Every time the demonic voices spoke through Jessica, a glaze seemed to come over her eyes and she took on an evil countenance which she did not normally have. As I prayed in the Spirit, that diabolic expression became more intense than ever. Her hate-filled eyes glared into mine and she pointed at me with her forefinger and little finger, the two middle fingers and her thumb curled under. I was later to learn this is a hex sign, used in casting spells and pronouncing curses. As she pointed, I was astounded to hear a man's voice speak clearly in a language I could not understand. Then, reverting back to English, the voice hissed, "See there, I can do it too. You don't have any power that I don't have."

Paul Dana and I both shuddered and ordered the demon to be quiet. Jessica came to herself again.

When the demons were not manifesting themselves through Jessica, she was a very subdued and gentle person with a sweet personality. Although the demonic voices swore and cursed repeatedly, I never heard Jessica use vulgar or profane language in her own voice.

I told Jessica this and asked if she was aware of the malevolent spirits which manifested themselves through her. I let her know that the demons were particularly roused whenever we mentioned the name of Jesus. She said she was not aware of the voices, but she felt that something strange was happening.

I told her I had a recorder with me and asked if she minded my taping our conversation. If she would allow me to do so, I would play the demon voices back to her if they should speak again. She agreed to this saying, "It won't bother me, but don't waste your tape."

Actually, the recorder was already running. I put in a fresh tape and Jessica continued, "What bothers me is that on All Hallows Eve, which is Halloween to you, when we conjure up spirits and they refuse to show their face or manifest themselves, we threaten them. We threaten them by God. I don't know why that is, but whenever we use the name of God, then immediately they manifest themselves."

"They are rebelling against Him," I explained. "They are so opposed to God that they can't stand the sound of His name."

I asked Jessica if she would repeat a simple five word prayer after me. "Jesus, reveal yourself to me." She agreed to try.

"Jesus," I prompted, and waited for her to follow.

Jessica's eyes grew wild and rolled back with a terrified look. Her chin and throat protruded but no sound came out of her opened mouth.

"Say it," I prodded, "Say Jesus."

A guttural belch came from somewhere deep inside her.

I repeated the phrase. "Say, Jesus, reveal yourself to me."

She tried again, but this time only a weak hiccup came from her throat.

The frightened look of a trapped animal was in her eyes as Jessica recoiled in her chair. That indescribable glaze came over her face and a deep whispered voice came from her lips, "Get away from me."

"Who are you?" I asked.

"You are a son of a bitch. Get away from me. Get away," the deep voice replied as Jessica pushed her chair further back against the wall.

"What is your name?" I demanded.

"Beluth," was the one word answer.

"And where do you come from?"

"Tartarus."

"And where is that?"

"Hell."

"Then, what are you doing here?"

"I belong here," Beluth hissed.

"You belong where?" I asked.

"In this girl."

"Why are you in this girl?

"Because of her grandfather?"

"And who is her grandfather?"

I was later to learn the demon's answer to this question was a lie. This simply goes to show that one cannot put much stock in the word of Satan, whom the Bible describes as "*a liar, and the father of it.*" John 8:44.

The voice said that the name of Jessica's grandfather was Anton LaVey. Many will recognize this name as the founder of the Church of Satan and author of *The Satanic Bible*.

I continued my questioning, "By what right does her grandfather allow you to possess this girl?"

"By a blood covenant," was the answer.

"A blood covenant between whom?"

"Between Satan, and himself, and Mephistopheles."

"And who is Mephistopheles?" I asked.

"The soul barterer," was the reply. Then, the voice asked, "What right have you to ask me these questions?"

My answer came quickly and with inspiration. "The right I have is that I am a child of the true and living God, possessed of his Holy Spirit, and bought by the blood of Jesus Christ at Calvary."

The voice spat back angrily, "You shut your mouth. I despise you."

"Yes," I answered, "You despise God and all that He stands for because you know that I ha ..."

The alien voice coming from Jessica's lips interrupted me defiantly in mid-sentence. "You will not help this girl. You will not help her. Do you understand me? You will not help her."

"Jesus will help her."

"No, he will not help her"

"The Holy Spirit will help her," I continued.

"No," came the demon's retreating word. Jessica's eyes closed, she blacked out, and slumped down into her chair.

When she revived a few minutes later, Jessica asked Paul Dana and me, "Why don't you just give up and go back home now?" She reminded us that it was check out time. We told her that wasn't important; we would pay for another day.

Jessica laughed, "I'm still trying to get through to the reality of this thing. I mean, you really are here, all the way from Augusta? It freaks me out."

I told Jessica the reason Paul Dana and I were there, taking our time and spending our money, was because we loved her. "Actually, not us, but Jesus Christ in us loves you," I said. "He lives in us."

As I spoke of Jesus, Jessica lapsed again into one of her trances. Paul Dana said "She's not here, Stephen." Then turning to Jessica, he called her name.

"Yeah, I'm here," she responded.

"Did you hear what he had to say?" Paul Dana asked.

"Yeah, I heard him."

"What did he say?"

Jessica answered, "He said that he's got somebody living inside of him."

"Who is it?" Paul Dana asked.

"I didn't catch the name."

"His name is Jesus," we both told her in unison, but we were not sure she heard us that time either. It seemed the forces of Hell stopped Jessica's ears every time the name of Jesus was mentioned. I remembered the scripture which says, "*The god of this world hath blinded the minds of them which believe not, lest the light of the glorious gospel of Christ, who is the image of God, should shine unto them.*" II Corinthians 4:4.

Once again, I asked Jessica if she would try to pray with us. "If Jesus Christ is God, and if he is real," I reasoned with her, "then you shouldn't be afraid to ask him to reveal himself to you."

Jessica told me that a psychic barrier kept her from repeating the prayer, but she agreed to try again. This time, I reversed the order of the prayer, thinking it might be easier for her. I asked her to repeat, "Reveal yourself to me, Jesus."

She said, "Reveal yourself to me …," then her eyes rolled back until little was showing but the white, and she belched.

We tried the same prayer several times, again with the same results. Finally, Jessica went into a deep trance in which she could not hear or respond to anything I said.

Paul Dana and I prayed a long prayer in which we rebuked Satan and demanded him to loose her. The demons manifested themselves repeatedly and each time we ordered them to be quiet and go in the name of Jesus and by the authority of his blood.

One of the demons which spoke during this time identified himself as Mephistopheles, the Soul Barterer. "Let's talk this over," he offered. We informed him we were not there to barter or bargain, but to cast him out. We said he had nothing he could offer for this girl because she had been purchased with the blood of Jesus. With that, Mephistopheles departed.

When Jessica finally came to herself again, she was physically exhausted. I mentioned the name of Jesus again and she sighed, "I know nothing about him, not really."

Hoping the demons would now allow her to listen, I began to explain again in elementary terms, "You see, Jessica, there are not many gods. There is only one true and living ..."

I was cut short by yet another male voice in a condescending tone, "I know that."

"I know that you know," I answered the demon, "But Jessica may not know."

"Let's keep it that way," the demon replied through her lips.

"You be quiet and let me speak to Jessica. Be gone in Jesus' name," I demanded firmly.

"Your time is running out," the demon persisted.

I informed the voice it was his time which was running out; that he was already defeated and he knew it.

"You haven't cast even one of us out yet," the demon taunted. "You're just wasting your time."

"But you know your time is limited and that is why you are trembling," I said.

"I'm not trembling," the guttural voice of the demon responded. The voice began to speak in a language which I could not understand and while in her trancelike state, with a heinous, beastly look in her eyes, Jessica pointed her index finger and little finger at me in the hex sign.

It was as though a sudden surge of faith flowed into Paul Dana and me. We felt the demons were afraid and desperate so we began to pray harder. At the same time, we rejoiced in the Lord and praised Him for the victory we felt sure would come soon.

As we prayed, Paul Dana and I were standing in the center of the room and Jessica was sitting in her chair against the wall. During the prayer, I closed my eyes for a moment out of habit. When I opened them again, I saw that Jessica had gotten up from her seat and was standing within inches of me. The demonic glare of her eyes pierced mine and I heard the growling curse of a malignant spirit's voice from her lips.

A cold chill swept up my spine and tingled out my arms to the fingertips. Jessica began to hit at me with her fists while she kicked in karate fashion at Paul Dana. We grabbed her arms to try to constrain her, but she jerked away. All the while, we were pleading the blood of Jesus. Finally, with an anguished moan, which sounded to me like the despairing wail of a lost soul sinking into Hell, Jessica fainted across the bed.

5

Jesus, Why Are You So Bright?

o o o o o o o o o o o o o o o o o o o o o o o o o

Then was brought unto him one possessed with a devil, blind, and dumb: and he healed him, insomuch that the blind and dumb both spake and saw.

—Matthew 12:22

We must remember that Satan has his miracles too.

—John Calvin 91509–1564)
French Protestant Theologian

Paul Dana and I had been so focused on Jessica and the demons we were trying to exorcise, I had forgotten I was making a tape recording of our conversation. As she was laying across the bed in a faint, I remembered and rewound the tape. When she came to herself again, I played back to Jessica one of the most uncanny of the demonic voices—that of Beluth.

Jessica listened with wide-eyed interest. She was incredulous, not quite sure what to make of the things she was hearing. She would not agree that the voices had come from her own lips and said that maybe we had just fabricated the whole thing. Still, the recording seemed to give Jessica a stronger interest in hearing what Paul Dana and I had to share with her.

We spent a long time explaining to Jessica the simple message of the Gospel. When I told her that Jesus died, giving his life as a sacrifice for her, she asked, "What did he do that for? My grandfather died for me. You mean there is a counterfeit?"

I explained that there was indeed a counterfeit sacrifice and it was the one made by her grandfather. Jesus' sacrifice was the genuine one by which God had purchased her soul.

It was well past noon now and we had been counseling and praying with Jessica for more than four hours. I asked her one last time if she would pray. I changed the prayer somewhat by asking her to repeat after me, "Jesus, come into my heart."

The demons manifested themselves quickly at this suggestion. "No, no," came a rasping demon voice. "That will never do. I would rather you say the other one."

"You mean the prayer, 'Jesus, reveal yourself to me?'"

"Yes, that's much better, don't you think?" the demon responded.

I can't imagine why Satan would make such a suggestion to me. Maybe he wasn't as smart as I had given him credit for being. Now, I knew the prayer the devil feared most. I ordered the demons to depart and instructed Jessica to repeat after me, "Jesus, come into my heart."

Jessica struggled gallantly for several seconds to say the name of Jesus. The best she could do was to get out the first syllable, followed by a hiccup or rattle in her throat. She prayed, "Jekkkk, come into my heart."

It was a simple five word prayer. Jessica had not been able to clearly say the name of Jesus. However, I felt that even though she could not articulate his name, in her soul, she had called out to Jesus to the best of her ability and he would hear her.

I asked Jessica to repeat the prayer. As she began to try, her personality suddenly changed and she jumped up from her chair in a rage. Demon voices cursed and swore through her and she began to attack us by hitting and kicking. Paul Dana and I both had heard Jessica invite Jesus into her heart and we sensed that deliverance was near. With renewed vigor and an increased sense of authority, we commanded the demons to go in the name of Jesus. After a few violent moments, Jessica passed out again. Paul Dana and I caught her and eased her down onto her chair.

As Jessica lay there in a stupor, the seven rings on her fingers grabbed my attention. The rings had been one of the first things I noticed upon meeting Jessica that morning. Now, it was as though the Holy Spirit impressed me that their power must be broken.

When she came to her senses, I asked Jessica what the rings meant.

"Oh, they are just rings," she said. One by one, she pulled them off and put them back on saying, "See, they don't really mean anything." Then, she hesitated and said, "Except this middle ring." On the middle finger of her left hand was a silver ring in the image of a skull.

"This ring," she explained, "represents the covenant of my grandfather's blood. I can take all of the other rings off but I can never remember having this ring off before."

I counseled, "Jessica, you have invited Jesus into your heart. You have accepted His blood sacrifice for your soul. Now you must take off the skull ring because the covenant with your grandfather's blood holds no more power over you."

I watched in awe as Jessica struggled to remove the skull ring. It slipped easily out to the tip of her finger and then, as if by some unseen force, the ring seemed to spring back into place. Several times this was repeated as she strained and grunted. Her face betrayed the agony of her soul. Finally, with a great shriek and painful sigh, she threw the ring across the room where it hit the wall, bounced, and came to rest on the bed. Jessica slumped back into her chair like a limp rag doll.

On the desk beside where I stood was a Gideon Bible. I had not planned this, but as if on cue, I felt impressed to hand it to her. I reached the Bible out toward Jessica and held it within easy arm's length. "Jessica," I said. "I'm not going to put this Bible in your lap, but I want you to take it for yourself, of your own free will."

Gesturing toward the ring lying on the bed, I said, "That ring represented the old covenant with Satan, sealed with your grandfather's blood. You have rejected that covenant. This book represents the covenant of the blood sacrifice of Jesus Christ. Take it, Jessica."

As I reached out the Bible toward her, the demon voices began to speak through her, but in a very different way than they had before. The voices were insistent, yet subdued. A normal expression was on Jessica's face as though it was she, and not the evil spirits, peering through her eyes. Although the voices were coming from her mouth, they seemed to have no control over her body. "No, no," they protested. "Don't take that book. Don't take it. It is all lies. It is all lies." This time, ignoring the voices, Jessica slowly reached out and touched the Bible with one finger, a second, a third, and finally clasped the book in her hand, taking it from mine.

As Jessica laid the Bible in her lap and opened it, the voices continued to protest, "Don't turn the pages. Don't turn the pages." But, she turned them none the less. She was looking ahead and not at the Bible as her fingers idly flipped the pages.

What happened next was so uncanny I would have a very difficult time believing it if I had not been there and seen it first hand. Jessica's hands stopped and her gaze shifted down to the Bible. The guttural voices from her own lips pleaded, "Don't read it. Don't read it."

I wanted to take the Bible and help Jessica find an appropriate scripture, but I felt the Holy Spirit constrained me. He was about to show me one of the most amazing miracles I have ever experienced. I heard Paul Dana say, "Read it, Jessica. Read it."

The sequence of scriptures read at random by this girl who knew practically nothing of the Bible was astonishing.

The demon voices were silent and Jessica's voice began reading slowly and deliberately from the first chapter of Romans: *"for I am not ashamed of the gospel of Christ: for it is the power of God unto salvation to every one that believeth...."* As she read, Paul Dana and I began to weep unashamedly.

Jessica read verses 16–25 of the first chapter of Romans and then, looking up from the Bible, she once again began to turn the pages. I was watching Jessica closely and saw that her gaze was transfixed as if in a trance. The voice of a demon again muttered in protest through her lips, "Don't turn the pages. Don't read any more of that book. It is lies. It is lies."

The voice retreated without our command and Jessica's finger stopped at Mark 16:9. She looked back down to the open Bible in her lap and read *"Now when Jesus was risen early the first day of the week, he appeared first to Mary Magdalene, out of whom he had cast seven devils."* She paused and skipped down to verse 17. *"And these signs shall follow them that believe; In my name they shall cast out devils; they shall speak with new tongues;"*

Jessica looked back up from the Bible, again in a detached state. Her hands continued to leaf through the Bible until they paused, this time at Ephesians 6. She looked down and read softly, *"Finally, my brethren, be strong in the Lord, and in the power of his might. Put on the whole armor of God that ye may be able to stand against the wiles of the devil. For we wrestle not against flesh and blood, but against principalities, against powers, against the rulers of the darkness of this world, against spiritual wickedness in high places."*

As before, Jessica turned more pages and stopped at Acts 20:28 to read how God's church had been *"… purchased with his own blood."*

Her fingers turned next to Psalm 91 where she read of the security and protection the believer finds in the Lord. From the Psalms, she flipped to Revelations 3:20 and read, *"Behold,*

I stand at the door, and knock: if any man hear my voice, and open the door, I will come in to him, and will sup with him, and he with me...."

Paul Dana and I looked on in astonishment as this amazing sequence of scriptures was read slowly and deliberately in Jessica's own sweet, soft voice. Every time Jessica turned the pages, she did not seem to even be looking at the Bible. Between each scripture, muffled demon voices begged her not to read any more.

After reading from the third chapter of Revelations, she paused and sat quietly, staring ahead as if in a daze. I spoke to her again, "Jessica, the evil spirits have gone. You said the name of Jesus. You invited Him into your life. You threw away the symbol of your old witchcraft covenant with your grandfather's blood, and you have read the new covenant of Jesus' blood."

I instructed her, "Your soul is cleansed. But now that the evil spirits have departed, you must invite the Holy Spirit to fill the empty place they have left so that there will never be any room for them to return and take up residence again."

I told her this because of the scripture which says, *"When the unclean spirit is gone out of a man, he walketh through dry places, seeking rest, and findeth none. Then he saith, I will return into my house from whence I came out; and when he is come, he findeth it empty, swept, and garnished. Then goeth he, and taketh with himself seven other spirits more wicked than himself, and they enter in and dwell there, and the last state of that man is worse than the first....."* Matthew 12:43–45.

Jessica said nothing in response. Still staring ahead, she began to leaf through the Bible one more time. It was as though some power other than her own was using her fingers to turn the pages as she stared blankly ahead. Demon voices protested again, "No, no, don't read it." But, the voices had no power to stop her from turning the pages. When she paused, her eyes dropped to Acts 1:8. She read aloud, *"But ye shall receive power, after that the Holy Ghost is come upon you: and ye shall be witnesses …"*

As she read about the Holy Spirit, I was surprised and dismayed to see her eyes take on an inexplicable crazed look and she went into a violent fit. Jessica sprang to her feet and with anguished groans began to rip and tear at the Bible as a hellish voice cried loudly through her, "No! No!"

Paul Dana and I rebuked the evil spirits and as we did, Jessica bucked and tossed as though being pummeled by some unseen force. She dropped the mutilated Bible to the floor and put her hands to the sides of her face as if in pain. Her head was thrown back; she let out a long, shrill, anguished cry, and then fell back onto her chair, face up.

Always when the demons manifested themselves through Jessica, her eyes were open, but now they were closed. There was a long moment of silence. Then, Jessica's lips parted and we heard her own weak, soft voice. Clearly and without constraint she whispered, "Jesus … Jesus … Jesus." It was the most beautiful sound I had ever heard.

Jessica continued her prayer, "Why are you so bright, Jesus? Why are you so bright?"

Paul Dana spoke, "He is the light of the world, Jessica."

There was another pause and she said, "I don't know much about you, Jesus. But I'm going to learn." And then, just for a few moments, she whispered softly in an unknown tongue as the Spirit gave her the utterance. How very different it was from the demonic language in which she had spoken earlier.

After Jessica completed her prayer and regained her composure, Paul Dana and I shared a scripture with her from Romans 10:9: *"That if thou shalt confess with thy mouth the Lord Jesus, and shalt believe in thine heart that God hath raised him from the dead, thou shalt be saved."*

We then led Jessica in a prayer of confirmation in which she declared, "Jesus is my Lord and Saviour. Satan is defeated and is no longer my master. Jesus is my only master."

I glanced at my watch; it was 2:00 PM. For almost six hours, we had battled the forces of darkness before the light had gloriously shone into that hotel room. I sighed in relief, feeling that the devil had been defeated. I was soon to learn he was only in retreat.

6

The Demons Return

Lest Satan should get an advantage of us: for we are not ignorant of his devices.

—2 Corinthians 2:11

Let us watch Satan, for he watcheth us. There is no corporeal enemy, but a man naturally fears; the spiritual foe appears less terrible, because we are less sensible of him.

—Thomas Adams (1583–1652)
Puritan Theologian

After Jessica's deliverance, Paul Dana and I knew she would have to return with us to Augusta for at least a few days. There was no reasonable alternative. To leave her alone would be the spiritual equivalent of a couple birthing a baby and then abandoning the infant to fend for herself. Jessica needed nurture, care, and a time to grow and mature in her new-found Christian faith.

That very night our church had chartered a bus to go to the Carolina Coliseum in Columbia, South Carolina, for a concert with Bill and Gloria Gaither. We told Jessica of the concert and used it as bait to lure her to return with us. She agreed under the condition we prepay her bus ticket back to Savannah and assure her that she would not be kidnapped or stranded in Augusta. We took her by the Greyhound terminal, bought the ticket, and started toward home.

As we were driving, I felt it would be a good time to begin giving Jessica some elementary instructions in living the Christian life. I quoted to her II Corinthians 5:17, *"Therefore if any man be in Christ, he is a new creature: old things are passed away; behold all things are become new."* I explained to Jessica that her old lifestyle and habits of witchcraft were now a thing of the past.

I instructed Jessica that there were four things which would help her as she began her new Christian walk: (1) prayer, (2) Bible reading, (3) worship, and (4) fellowship.

As I talked, I noticed that Jessica grew strangely silent and fidgety. She sat in the front seat beside me and Paul Dana was in the back. I glanced at Jessica's face and was horrified to see the same glassy, satanic expression which she had manifested earlier in the hotel room. Had the demons returned? Had they never been fully exorcised in the first place?

These questions raced through my mind as we were traveling toward Augusta at about fifty-five miles per hour. Suddenly, Jessica jerked the car door open as if to jump out.

Just as quickly, Paul Dana grabbed Jessica from behind. I also gripped Jessica's left arm and we firmly commanded the demons to depart. Jessica shook her head as if being startled awake from sleep as she returned to her normal self. Paul Dana reached over the seat, closed, and locked the car door.

This incident was beyond my understanding. Jessica's experience in the hotel room just an hour earlier had been so beautiful—so real. Or had it been real? After her deliverance, we had plainly heard Jessica renounce Satan and all his emissaries. She had invited Jesus into her heart and had confessed that Jesus alone was her Lord and Master.

According to everything I had ever believed and preached, demons cannot possess a child of God. Had I been wrong? Was Jessica really God's child? The answers to these questions would have to wait. For now, I would change our conversation to safer subjects. I could not risk antagonizing the evil spirits while we were driving.

When we arrived back in Augusta, it was too late to catch the bus to the Gaither concert. I had called our Minister of Music, Ruth Garrard, and asked her to go ahead without us rather than cause forty-five people to be late.

When we arrived home, a few members of the college/career class from our church were just leaving from their long prayer vigil. One of the young men, Grady Mosley, volunteered to take my wife, Jessica, and me to the concert in his car. It seemed a coincidence that we happened to have an extra ticket for Grady. We would soon see that it was no coincidence at all, but Divine providence. Grady was to play a vital part in Jessica's complete deliverance.

The concert was beautiful, as the Gaithers always are. However, I was unable to enjoy the music for fear of Jessica's reaction. If it had not been for the incident when she tried to jump out of the car, I would not have been concerned at all. But now, I didn't know what to expect.

Jessica was very restless throughout the concert. Twice she got up and went out to smoke. On the way home that evening, she lay down in the front seat of the car and went to sleep. Pat and I were sitting in the back.

After she had been sleeping for half an hour, Jessica began to squirm fitfully and talk in her sleep. "No, no they're going to kill me. Don't let them kill me. Don't let them kill me!"

I reached over the seat, laid my hand gently on her shoulder, and began to pray softly for God to take away the nightmare and let her rest. Pat prayed with me and as she did, she laid a Bible on Jessica's side. Jessica, who could not have seen the Bible to know what it was, recoiled violently and groaned as if she had been touched by a hot iron.

I could hardly believe what I had just seen. The Bible is not some kind of magic charm. There is no power in the leather and paper. The power is in the words as they are applied to our hearts. Jessica was apparently asleep and her eyes were tightly closed. Even if she had been awake, it is hardly possible she could have known it was a Bible which touched her. Yet, her reaction to the touch of that sacred book was unmistakable.

The next morning was Sunday and we woke Jessica in time to ask if she would like to go to church with us. She declined our invitation, saying she felt sick to her stomach. We thought it would be unwise to leave her in our house alone, so we called a mature, Spirit-filled couple from our congregation and asked if they would miss church to stay with Jessica.

Jessica resented the "babysitters" and told us so when we returned home. She had refused to speak to them and had spent most of the morning sitting alone on a picnic table out beside the pond behind our house.

We had lunch on our back deck as it was a mild spring day. While we were eating, I noticed an inch-long crowfoot scar, the symbol of a perverted cross, on Jessica's wrist. It was festered and red. The day before, while in Savannah, Jessica had told Paul Dana and me that the scar was the result of a witchcraft ritual and it had refused to heal properly.

On an impulse, I asked Jessica if I could pray. I reached out and lightly touched the crowfoot saying, "Jessica, God can cause this infection to heal completely. Jesus is not only our Saviour but also our Healer. As he causes this inflammation to clear up, it will be a demonstration to you that the power of God is greater than the power of witchcraft."

As I began to pray, a demonic expression of hatred flashed through Jessica's eyes. She yanked her arm away from me. A demon's voice spoke through her, "No, no, don't do that. Leave it alone."

I was shocked. After our experience in the Savannah hotel the day before, I didn't expect to ever hear the demons speak through Jessica again. It was the first time Pat had heard the demons speak except over the telephone. I had been very concerned over all of Jessica's actions since our trip back to Augusta, but this disturbed me most of all. I just couldn't understand it. In a hushed voice, I rebuked the demon and

Jessica returned to her senses. As we finished our lunch, I silently prayed that God would teach me all I needed to know in dealing with the situation.

Later that afternoon, I gave Jessica one of my extra copies of the Bible. I mentioned the beautiful experience in which she had read the scriptures after seeing the bright light the day before. Jessica talked much of that light. She said it was one of the most real things she had ever experienced and that she had never seen anything so beautiful in all of her years of witchcraft.

I let Jessica know that she had been particularly blessed to have seen the bright light. Such a phenomenon has occurred before, as with Saul of Tarsus, who became the Apostle Paul, on the road to Damascus. But, seeing a bright light is not the experience of most people who encounter the living God. I explained it was by faith alone she had received salvation. For reasons known only to God, by His sovereign power and grace, he had allowed her to glimpse the brightness of his glory.

Jessica said she only had a vague memory of reading the scriptures in Savannah after seeing the light. When I turned to some of the passages and read them aloud to her, she said she did not recall having heard them before. Perhaps this miracle had been as much for Paul Dana and me as it had been for Jessica.

She asked me if the Bible had anything to say about witchcraft. I assured her that it did and turned to Deuteronomy 18:10–12. Sitting on the couch beside Jessica, I handed her the open Bible, and she began to read. *"There shall not be*

*found among you any one that maketh his son or his daughter to
pass through the fire, or that useth divination, or an observer of
times, or an enchanter, or a witch, or a charmer, or a consulter
with familiar spirits, or a wizard, or a necromancer. For all that
do these things are an abomination unto the Lord."*

On her first attempt, Jessica read only the first few words of
these verses and stopped. I took the Bible and continued to
read aloud. As I did, a demonic personality took control of her
and began to curse and swear. It was immediately obvious that
the angry voice I heard was not that of Jessica.

"Who are you?" I asked.

"Moloch," came the reply.

"Didn't I cast you out of this girl yesterday?"

"Yes, but we have returned," the demon snarled. "You
puny man of God, you have no power over us." I'm sure the
demon didn't realize it, but that statement from Moloch
encouraged me greatly. I already knew I was puny, and now
the devil recognized me as a "man of God." I felt compli-
mented, in the same sense as the late Leonard Ravenhill who
once said, *"My main ambition in life is to be on the devil's most
wanted list."*

Still, my mind was full of questions. Had the demons actually repossessed Jessica or were they merely trying to do so?
Possession denotes ownership, I reasoned. If Jessica had given
her heart to God and he now possessed her soul, then I
thought it would be impossible for Satan to also possess her.
Could it be that Jessica was actually a child of God and this
was a case of demonic oppression? If so, Satan's power to
oppress a Christian was much greater than I had ever thought.

Theological questions and implications would have to wait. Right now, there was a tormented young woman on my couch who was in need of deliverance.

The demon spoke again. "We will not let her hear the word of God. We made her sick so she would not go to church this morning."

Once again, the stupid demons, in an effort to show their power, had blown their cover. I laid my hands on Jessica and claimed her healing. As I prayed, I forbade Satan to afflict her or in any way to prevent her from going to church with us that evening.

The voices protested as if in agony. "No, no, she can't go. If she goes to church tonight then we will all have to come out."

"But she will go," I declared. "You cannot stop her."

"That's right," the demon voice whimpered. "We can no longer control her." Jessica came to herself, got up, and began getting ready to go with us to the Sunday evening service.

Our youth pastor, Paul Dana, was scheduled to preach that night. I called and warned him to be prepared in case of a disturbance during the service. I fully expected it to come. However, God had other plans.

I kept a close eye on Jessica throughout the service. She was fidgety, but that was all. God spared us from any public demonstration or unpleasant incident. I still believed that God had something special in store for Jessica before the evening was over. In that, I would not be disappointed.

7

I Am Lucifer

o o o o o o o o o o o o o o o o o o o o o o o o o o

How art thou fallen from heaven, O Lucifer, son of the morning! how art thou cut down to the ground, which didst weaken the nations!

—Isaiah 14:12

Pandemonium, the high capital/Of Satan and his peers.

—John Milton (1608–1674)
English Poet and Historian

Upon returning home from the Sunday evening church service, my wife and I immediately took our three sons upstairs to their rooms and put them to bed. We were thankful when they went to sleep that evening earlier than usual.

Our oldest son's bedroom was connected to the downstairs den with an open heating and air-conditioning vent. Sounds traveled through that vent almost as if they were in the same room. Yet Gregory slept soundly, not hearing any of the repeated piercing screams which would punctuate the night until almost sunrise on Monday morning. The screams that night would be much louder than even those Paul Dana and I heard in the hotel room in Savannah. We feared our neighbors would hear them and call the police, yet our boys slept soundly.

It started around 10:00 PM when Jessica suggested we read some more together from the Bible. She was especially interested in learning more of what the Bible had to say about witchcraft.

I turned to the passage we had tried to read earlier that afternoon, Deuteronomy 18:10–12. Jessica had borrowed one of my wife's robes and was sitting on the couch beside us. Before Jessica finished reading even the first verse, a gruff man's voice bellowed from her lips, "No!" At that, she jumped up and ran out the front door of our house and into the street.

My first impulse was to go after her. However, I felt a check in my spirit, so I just stood on the front porch and watched as she walked up the middle of the street in my wife's robe. When she rounded the corner and went out of sight, I returned to the den and prayed, leaving the front door open and the porch light on. In about fifteen minutes, Jessica came back into the house. She said she did not remember going out.

About the time Jessica returned, the telephone rang. It was Grady Mosley, the young man who had taken us to the Gaither concert the night before. He was calling Jessica to wish her good night and to let her know he was praying for her.

As Jessica was speaking to Grady, her voice suddenly changed to that of a snarling demon, cursing and raving loudly. She threw the telephone down onto the carpet in a rage—screaming, clawing, and kicking. Jessica was so violent that the only way I could constrain her was to wrestle her to the floor.

Pat grabbed the phone and told Grady to bring Paul Dana and get to our house as fast as they could. She then joined me in kneeling over Jessica and praying. I heard Pat behind me saying to the demons which were manifesting themselves through Jessica, "I rebuke you in Jesus' name."

Jessica's hate-filled glare shot past me toward Pat and a deep, indignant man's voice hissed, "I'll leave this girl, but I will not leave this house."

Pat thought of our three young sons asleep upstairs and of the home we both loved so much. With a rare boldness that surprised both of us, she retorted, "Yes, you will leave, because the blood of Jesus Christ covers this house."

"Why are you trying to help this girl anyway?" the demon asked defiantly. "You don't even know who she is. Her real name is not Jessica."

I told the demon I was not surprised and it did not matter what her name was. Then, I asked, "How many more of you are there?"

"Many, many," came the answer. "You would be surprised how many."

"In Jesus' name," I ordered, "you must tell me how many more of you there are."

"Two thousand, eight hundred and seventy-six," the impish voice replied.

"And what are your names?" I demanded.

In rapid succession, a long list of occult terms spat from Jessica's lips, "Ouija boards, divination, tarot cards, crystal balls, tea leaves …" and more.

As quickly as the words came from Jessica's mouth, I repeated them and then laid my hand on her forehead commanding, "I cast you out in the name of Jesus. I bind your power and forbid you ever to return to this girl again."

The voice replied sarcastically, "We'll go, but we are only the principalities. You'll never get all of us." And at that, Jessica's eyes rolled back and her body bucked and stiffened. She put her hands up to her temples as if in great pain, let out a long, loud piercing scream, and blacked out.

I let Jessica lie motionless on the floor for a few minutes while I rested from the ordeal, praying all the while for guidance as to what to do next.

When Jessica came to herself, I offered her a hand to help her up off the floor and back onto the couch. At that moment, Pat looked out the window and saw Paul Dana and Grady turn into our driveway. She went to the front door and stepped out onto the porch to bring them up to date on what was happening before they came into the house. As she did, Jessica got up and locked the door with them on the outside. She came back into the den without saying a word, but with the most heinous, wild-eyed demonic expression yet. I felt I was seeing pure evil in her eyes.

"Who are you?" I asked.

In a deep, gruff voice, a demon announced through her lips, "I am Lucifer!"

Jessica grabbed me by the throat and began to choke me. I was surprised at her strength. With great effort, I pried her hands from my neck, pinning her arms to her side. In the ruckus, the two of us hit the floor rolling as she kicked and growled. Meanwhile, Pat, Paul Dana, and Grady had gone all the way around the house, trying every door and finding them all locked. As Jessica and I wrestled on the floor, the three of them were jumping up and down in the flower bed outside the den window, pleading the blood of Jesus.

Whether it was really Lucifer or just another lying demon manifesting himself through Jessica at that moment, I do not know. After several minutes of intense struggle, Jessica finally let out that heinous, piercing scream which we would hear many times before the night was through. As the demon departed, I declared that he was bound and ordered him in the name of Jesus to never return again.

Jessica collapsed. I left her lying on the floor and went to open the front door.

With the prayer support of Paul Dana and Grady, we determined we would not stop our efforts that night until we had an assurance from God that Jessica was totally delivered. Although the manifestations were just as sinister and violent—even more so—than they had been the morning before in Savannah, Jessica herself was a very different person in between the demonic episodes. She readily acknowledged that she had rejected witchcraft and that Jesus was her Lord. She said that she knew she was different, but there was still something inside which she described as knots in her stomach. Jessica asked us, "If you cast these things out of me yesterday morning, then why are they still here, and why do the demons still have control of me?" I was asking myself the same questions.

We could not give Jessica an answer but we pointed out that great progress and improvement had been made. We assured her we would just keep on trusting God until her deliverance was complete.

Since the demons manifested themselves twice before when we had started to read the scriptures which forbid witchcraft, I thought that would be the area to which we should pay attention. I explained to Jessica that we would try to read the scriptures again. If the demons should manifest themselves, we would make each of them identify themselves and cast them out, binding them, and forbidding them ever to return.

Jessica expressed fear that the demons might harm her. Yet, her reluctance to cooperate was overcome by her desperate desire to be free. She took the Bible I had given her and began to read. Halfway through the first scripture, her voice changed to that of an older woman and her expression to that indescribable demonic glaze. I asked, "Who are you?"

"Kali," came the reply. I was to later learn Kali is the name of a Hindu high priestess and daughter of Shiva, "the destroyer."

I asked Kali how many she represented, or how many subordinate demons were under her control.

"There are more than two hundred of us," the voice of Kali replied.

We began to rebuke these demons in the name of Jesus. As we did, Jessica repeated the agonizing motions of putting her hands to her temples, throwing back her head, giving that hair-raising demonic scream, and fainting. This scene would be repeated at least a score of times before the night was over.

I felt the screams were the departing cries of demonic entities who did not want to leave, but were forced to go by the power of Jesus' blood. This reaction closely paralleled the Biblical instance of deliverance recorded in Mark 1:26, *"And when the unclean spirit had torn him, and cried with a loud voice, he came out of him."*

Each time another group of demons would be cast out, Jessica would faint. We would allow her to remain in her sleep-like state for a few minutes while we regathered our strength and prayed. Each ordeal was exhausting. But, we noted with encouragement that each time Jessica read, she went a little further in the scriptures before the demons would manifest themselves again.

Demons with names such as Astaroth, Aristophanes, Spirit of the Druids, and Jezebel went out. They all departed with varying numbers of subordinate demons. When speaking to a demon voice, I would occasionally ask, "How many more of you possess this girl?" Each time the number given us would be smaller than before.

Finally, Jessica read the three verses from Deuteronomy in their entirety without interruption. However, I noticed she read somewhat differently than before. Every time I had heard Jessica read in her own voice, even on that beautiful occasion in the hotel room two mornings earlier, she had read slowly and deliberately, stumbling over her words, as if she were on about a third or fourth grade reading level. This time, she read precisely—rapidly. My first thought was that the demons had previously prevented her from reading as a normal twenty-three year old and now they had lost their ability to hinder her.

Jessica kept reading faster and faster, verse after verse. I realized it was not Jessica's voice at all, but that of another young woman. I turned to look into Jessica's eyes and there was no mistaking the diabolic expression. A demon had actually taken control and was reading the Bible through her.

I interrupted with the question, "Who are you?"

Jessica turned to me with one of the most mocking expressions I have ever seen. Her cheeks puffed out as if she were doing everything she could to keep from bursting into laughter.

"Who are you?" I demanded.

Her mouth opened wide in a cackling laugh. She pointed her finger at me and leaned back, then doubled over in a fit of hilarity. Her expression was so comical I had to bite my lip to keep from laughing myself, despite the lateness of the hour and the seriousness of the moment.

"In Jesus' name, tell me who you are!" I demanded again.

The demon's voice squealed loudly, "Mockery." Once again, Jessica pointed her finger at me and burst into a fit of demonic laughter.

The four of us who were with Jessica began to rebuke this demon spirit. Ignoring our rebukes, Jessica continued to laugh at us as though her sides would split, pointing in gleeful derision, first to one of us and then to another.

It was difficult to remain serious in the face of such hilarity. We were tempted to laugh with her and at the same time tempted to become angry because she was pointing and laughing at us. After several minutes of persistent prayer, Jessica's expression changed from hilarity to fear and the demons of mockery departed with a great cry of anguish.

After Jessica revived from her faint this time, she picked up the glass from which she had been drinking iced tea and went into the kitchen. I thought nothing of it since she was a perfectly normal and docile person between the times when the demons manifested themselves. Two or three times during these breaks she would plead, "Please be patient with me. I'm trying. Please don't give up until all of them come out."

Because of this, I had no reason to expect what happened next. Looking up from where we sat in the den, we saw Jessica standing in the kitchen. She held a butcher knife in her hand with the point of the sharp eight inch blade indenting her throat. Her crazed demonic eyes expressed fear and desperation.

Paul Dana and I immediately walked into the kitchen. Pat and Grady came behind us. I could hear them calling on the name of Jesus as I asked the demon his name.

A defiant male voice replied, "I am Suicide," and Jessica's arm that held the knife tensed.

I felt the blood drain from my face. Hoping my voice did not betray my anxiety, I said, "Suicide, I rebuke you in the name of Jesus and I forbid you to harm this girl."

"No," the harsh male voice withstood me. "I am going to kill her! I am going to end it all right here on your kitchen floor!"

Was this to be the end of our satanic ordeal, now entering its sixth day? Were all of our prayers going to end with the corpse of a young woman we did not even know, in a pool of her own blood, on our kitchen floor at three o'clock in the morning? How would we explain it to the police? What would we say to our church members?

If it is possible, we prayed now more earnestly than ever and demanded the demon of suicide to loose Jessica and let her live.

I was totally unprepared for what happened next. Jessica took the knife from her throat and with a sinister gleam in her eye, pointed it threateningly toward me, taking a step in my direction. I wanted very much to back away and tell the others to get out the back door. At the same time, I felt that would be the worst thing to do because it would show a lack of faith. There was no room to doubt at this stage of the game.

I asked again, "And who are you?"

"Murder," the demon voice hissed as Jessica took another step toward me, the demonic eyes coming through her fixed on mine. The arm which hoisted the knife tensed up as if it were a spring.

Whispering "Jesus help me," I closed the gap between Jessica and me with one quick step, reaching out to grab her hand which welded the knife. I fully expected to have to wrestle the knife away from her. However, at the very moment I touched Jessica's wrist, she dropped the knife and her whole body went limp in a faint. I caught her and Paul Dana helped me lower Jessica to the floor, being careful to kick the butcher knife aside so she would not lay on it.

After Jessica revived, we led her back into the den and continued reading the scriptures. We looked up every passage which has to do with witchcraft and several which pertained to demon possession, in both the Old and New Testaments. We were never able to read far before some demon entity would manifest itself.

One group of demons identified themselves as the Leek clan, headed by Demetrius Leek. The voices gave about a dozen other names. This was somewhat puzzling to us since Leek was not Jessica's real name but an alias which she used as a witch. There could be many explanations. The demons could have lied about their names and numbers. They could have chosen the name of Leek for whatever reason, or these could have been evil spirits which formerly possessed someone by the name of Leek and took on that identity. Whatever the case, the legion of Leek went out with a great cry just like all the rest.

Many of the demons identified themselves by the names of various sins or negative personality traits. This went against some of my theology—in fact many things that happened contradicted my theological understanding—but I am only reporting here the testimony of what we experienced. It is not my purpose to explain it all.

When a demon with a sultry feminine voice identified herself as Lust, Jessica began to nuzzle up to me, look dreamily into my eyes, and rub her hand up and down my arm. My wife seemed especially determined in helping cast this one out.

After a short while, the demon called Lust turned her attention to Grady—single and handsome—touching him and calling him by name in a very seductive voice. Grady responded only by joining the rest of us in rebuking the demon until it departed.

I teased Grady about this incident. In all of our dealings with the demon spirits, the only time one of them called any of us by name was then. I told him that he should feel honored that the devil knew his name. It reminded me of the scripture where a demon spoke to a group of hapless, would-be exorcists: *"And the evil spirit answered and said, Jesus I know, and Paul I know; but who are ye? And the man in whom the evil spirit was leaped on them, and overcame them, and prevailed against them, so that they fled out of that house naked and wounded."* Acts 19:15–16.

A demon by the name of Depression threw Jessica into the most vivid state of melancholy I have ever witnessed. Her posture drooped, her countenance was all washed out, and she seemed so weak she could barely speak. When a female demon called Sadness revealed herself, Jessica's face grew long like a hound dog and she began to softly cry, tears trickling down her cheeks.

Another demon said that his name was Lying. I asked how many he represented and the voice answered curtly, "Two."

I insisted, "In Jesus' name, you must tell me the truth. How many are you?" This time the demon voice confessed that he represented more than one hundred.

We reminded ourselves that every demon is a liar and nothing that a demonic voice says should be taken as absolute truth. Certainly no doctrine about the devil should be based in whole or part upon the word of demons. The Bible alone is the Christian's basis for doctrine.

One demon manifested himself but was reluctant to give his name. When I asked, the voice said, "I'll tell you later." Upon our insistence, this demon finally answered, "Procrastination." Then, when we demanded him to depart, the voice said, "Not now, I'll leave later. Okay?" By the authority of our Lord Jesus Christ, we would not permit Procrastination to stay a minute longer. He screamed and left as had all the others.

Several other demons departed that night, giving themselves such names as Hopelessness, Confusion, Incest, Anger, Self-Pity, Revenge, Lesbianism, and Hatred. Others had proper names such as Joziah, Aradia, and Lystophales. Since I am unfamiliar with these names and they were given orally, I am uncertain about their spelling.

Finally, we got to the place where we could read every scripture in the Bible about Witchcraft and demon possession without an adverse reaction from Jessica. Yet, she said there were still knots in her stomach, albeit not nearly so many as before.

After a long six hour ordeal, all of us were physically and emotionally exhausted. Jessica went to sleep on the couch. Paul Dana, Grady, and I were determined that we would not stop until, in some way, God had assured us that Jessica was completely delivered. We gathered around her sleeping form on the couch and prayed that God would revive Jessica and renew her strength, as well as our own.

As we prayed, Jessica stirred, yawned, and sat up wide awake. We also felt renewed strength surge through us. Thus began what turned out to be the longest and most difficult prayer of the evening.

Sensing total victory was near, we prayed incessantly and with fervor that every demon, named and unnamed, known and unknown, numbered and unnumbered, manifested and hidden, would come out in the name of Jesus, never to return again. As we prayed, tenacious demon spirits would occasionally manifest themselves briefly and then retreat, without being cast out.

Twice during the prayer we paused long enough to give each other encouragement and remind ourselves that we must not depend upon our own power, upon any magic formula, or upon a certain set of words. We must not just say the name of Jesus; we must invoke his power if we were to have complete victory.

It was after about twenty minutes of such concentrated prayer that the last stronghold of demons seemed to physically attack Jessica in the greatest struggle of the whole long ordeal. They pummeled Jessica's body as she squirmed and jerked and groaned. Foul curses and ranting came from her mouth until a white froth showed around her lips.

Jessica's glassy, hate-filled eyes fixed on Grady and as they did, he stepped forward and laid his hand on her forehead saying, "In Jesus' name." At that moment, her expression changed from hate to one of panic mixed with agony. She lifted her hands to the side of her face, threw back her head, and screamed so loud and long I felt surely she would wake the neighborhood. It was like the last despairing wail of the damned being cast into outer darkness. Jessica fainted and fell across the couch.

All of us collapsed either into our seats or onto the floor. The very atmosphere of the room seemed charged with electricity. Something was wonderfully different. The heavy feeling of oppressiveness had lifted; lightness was in the air. We felt a peace that passed understanding. I can't explain it, but we knew that Jessica was totally free. There was no doubt.

As Jessica lay unconscious on the couch, we began to laugh. Tears of joy mixed with our laughter. Someone shouted, "Praise the Lord!" We all looked at each other and just sat on the floor and laughed, and cried, and laughed, and cried, and praised the Lord together.

8

On Holy Ground

o o o o o o o o o o o o o o o o o o o o o o o o o o o

And it shall come to pass in the last days, saith God, I will pour out of my Spirit upon all flesh: and your sons and your daughters shall prophesy, and your young men shall see visions, and your old men shall dream dreams:

—*Acts 2:17*

I often laugh at Satan, and there is nothing that makes him so angry as when I attack him to his face, and tell him that through God I am more than a match for him.

—*Martin Luther (1483–1546)*
German Priest and Reformer

Whether Jessica had a dream or a vision, I do not know. Paul Dana, Grady, Pat, and I were very much awake on the den floor. Jessica lay sprawled on the couch where she had fainted, with the middle cushion knocked to the floor. Her arms clutched a pillow close to her bosom in teddy bear fashion. Her eyes were closed as if asleep.

As we were laughing and crying and rejoicing, I looked at Jessica and noticed that her lips were moving. She seemed to be saying "Jesus," but I could not hear her.

Paul Dana must have noticed also and ordered everyone to be quiet. Jessica's lips moved again and in a soft, barely audible voice, we heard her call her master's name. "Jesus? Jesus?" she said in a questioning tone that seemed to ask, "Is that you I see, Jesus?"

Continuing as though her question had been answered, she whispered, "I love you, Jesus. I praise you, Jesus."

After a short pause, we heard her inquire, "Jesus, why do you have holes in your hands? Nobody ever told me you had holes in your hands."

The four of us looked at each other in open-mouthed amazement. Paul Dana and I had told Jessica that Jesus died and made a blood sacrifice for her, but we had not gone into detail about the cross or the nails in his hands. Wells of tears sprang from our eyes. The whole room was charged with spiritual energy. Glory bumps tingled my arms and the back of my neck. I sensed an invisible holy company around us. If I had not already been in my stocking feet, I would have taken my shoes off because, for the next hour, the carpet in our den became holy ground.

Paul Dana and Grady both sensed we were about to hear more so they found pen and paper. Until five o'clock in the morning, we listened in amazement while they wrote the words that Jessica spoke. Her eyes were closed as if in sleep—very different than the trancelike state she had been in when the demons had manifested themselves through her. It was a conversation between Jessica and Jesus to which we were only permitted to hear the voice of Jessica. I felt that God in his sovereign grace was giving her a cram course to make up for the twenty-three years of her life in which she had been robbed of learning anything about Jesus. The Lord himself seemed to take her by the hand and lead her for a tour through his word.

After asking about the holes in Jesus' hands, she said, "You can tell me.… You have long hair too.… You have dark skin? … Are you Jewish?"

There were long pauses between Jessica's words. "You're eating? … What are you eating? … Bread and wine? … Does the wine have alcohol in it? … New Wine! … What kind of bird? … Is it a dove? … What's it doing on your shoulder?" Then, Jessica spoke softly for a few moments in an unknown tongue.

Could she have had a vision of Jesus in the garden tomb next? We heard her say, "What? … It's an angel inside watching over you in the room? … And a stone cast aside.… Up in the air … Oh! You went to Hell first and then to Heaven." Following these words, she spoke again for a short while in another language.

Next, the Lord seemed to show Jessica the road to Calvary. We heard her soft childlike voice, "What? … What are you going to do that for? … What are you riding on a donkey for?"

This was followed by another very long pause, after which Jessica continued: "It's almost time.… You have to go away?

... For how long? ... You will leave what here? ... Holy Spirit?" Then, as if imploring him to stay, she said, "You don't have to go."

Jessica's face and voice then showed great anguish, although her eyes remained tightly shut. "What are they doing? ... What is that man carrying that cross for? ... Cy ... Cyrene?" At this moment, she flinched and groaned.

"Don't fall, Jesus! ... Jesus, I love you," she said with compassion. Next she asked, "You are doing it for me? ... Who are those two people? ... One's going and one's not? ... He thinks he is better than you? ... I want to be the robber and go with you."

Much anguish was in Jessica's voice now as she continued, "What! ... He didn't do anything! ... Let me go instead! ... I'm the one who deserves to go, not you.... Oh God! Oh God! Oh God! He didn't do anything."

"Why is the water and blood coming from your side, Jesus? ... Your feet too? ... No! Y'all leave Him alone! ... You don't have to bargain for his clothes. What are you doing this for? He didn't hurt you."

The tone of Jessica's voice turned to puzzlement as she asked, "It's okay? ... You're going to do it because you want to? ... Your Father said it was okay and you want to do it? ... But it hurts!"

There was another long pause.

Jessica continued softly, "You're so bright.... I love you, Jesus; you died for me.... I know it hurt and now you're alive.... You didn't stay dead did you? ... I know.... Uh huh."

"Be what? … Fishers of men! … That don't make sense.… Oh! … You plant the seed and it grows—right? … So you give them the bait and they eat it—right? … Why are you doing this for me? … You wanted to show me? … Cause you love me?"

Next, Jessica sounded as though she were repeating after Jesus. Slowly and deliberately she recited, "Perfect love casts out all fear.… Be strong in the Lord and in the power of His might and put on the whole armor of God that you may be able to stand against the wiles of the devil."

These two sentences were direct quotes from the Bible, the last one being from the sixth chapter of Ephesians. Imagine our amazement when she said, "I can use that? … What? … Eph … Ephes … Ephesians six.… I can fight them just like David? Oh, it's not the big ones that are the problem, it's the little ones."

We felt Jessica's next words were directed at Satan as she recoiled and spoke in a sterner voice, "I'm not afraid of you."

Her voice softened again. "He did what? … He fell out of the sky? … And you put him under the feet.… Thank you, Jesus."

Jessica seemed to sleep for a few minutes, then began to speak again. "You're going to do what? … Take my asthma away? … Okay." She took a deep breath and let it out with a contented sigh as a big smile wrapped itself across her face.

During the time Jessica had been staying with us in Augusta, she was a strict vegetarian. Her next words were, "You mean I can if I want to? … I can eat meat if I want to?

... It's my choice? ... But it tastes bad.... Oh, you'll fix it.... I don't know yet if I want to."

We can only imagine what the Lord told Jessica next as she responded. "Do what? ... You're not going to let them do that are you? ... I can't do that! ... Oh, I can do all things through Christ who strengthens me.... I'll do it if you say so.... You tell me what to say."

Jessica started talking about her friends and parents and asked Jesus to keep them from going further into the things of Satan. Then, as if the Lord were teaching her, we heard her say, "Do what? ... What do you mean? ... Int ... Inter ... Intercede for them? ... You mean stand in proxy? ... I know you can do it."

"Don't go away! ... Stay here a few minutes.... Oh, you're not going.... You're going to stay.... Do what? ... I know.... Okay." She spoke again for a few moments in another language after which she paused and said in English, "Comforter?"

Jessica prayed next for her friends, calling many of them by name and forgiving some of them for wrongs they had done to her. Then she prayed, "Lord, forgive me for leading Tommy _____ astray into the paths of witchcraft for money's sake. I didn't mean to do it.... Do you forgive me? ... Oh, that's why you died!"

"What? ... Yes, I promised you that.... I'll do it tomorrow ... I know you'll be watching.... I know."

We shuddered as we heard Jessica say, "I claim _____ _____ that his mob will not mess up the Savannah Country

Club. And Lord, cancel my contract out on _____'s life to kill him. I'm sorry for starting it."

After another long pause, Jessica queried, "You're going to do what? … Take my ulcer away?" With a childlike trust in her voice, she said, "Thank you, Jesus."

God seemed to give Jessica a glimpse of the Old Testament next as she murmured, "You did what? … What's that bunch of people doing in the desert? … What did they eat? … Manna! … What's that? … Some kind of bread? … Okay."

She lapsed into an intimate time of worship in a tone that sounded like a little girl snuggling in her father's lap. "I love you, Jesus. I praise you, Jesus. I love you Lord Jesus Christ.… Father God Almighty. Father God Almighty.… I like that; I need a daddy."

Next, Jessica seemed to see Mary Magdalene. "Who is that washing your feet? … She's got pretty hair, long and black like mine.… Can I wash your feet? … I would if I could.… Why are they yelling at her? … They think they are better than she is? … Oh, but she serves you best because she loves you more."

Another long pause was followed by, "What do you mean, I'm a church? … Oh, like a temple.… By being a temple—your temple? … Oh, I like being a temple."

Jesus seemed to teach Jessica a primary lesson in prayer as we heard her say, "Okay, show me." Then, she slowly and deliberately recited the Lord's Prayer.

Jessica had been speaking very slowly with frequent pauses. Her conversation with the Lord up to this point had lasted for about thirty minutes. Paul Dana and Grady had both been writing her words as she spoke. I wanted to get my cassette recorder and try to catch what she was saying, but at the same time, I was afraid I might miss something. Also, I never would have expected her vision to last so long. As she repeated the Lord's Prayer, I ran to get my recorder. We caught the last half of her conversation on tape.

Jessica's next words were "You're coming again? ... Jesus is coming soon. Maybe night and maybe noon.... I don't know.... Gold.... And horses.... What kind of seal? ... Seven seals? ... The seven churches? ... And candle sticks? ... What?" After a pause, Jessica laughed and said, "Hey, that's neat."

Her next question was, "Where did you come from? ... A star? ... No, not a star. You were found by the star—by the people walking around.... What? ... You slept in a barn? ... Who was it? ... Mary.... Well, how did she get it? ... Was she married?" Jessica sighed deeply, "Ooohhh! Don't ever do that to me."

"I love you, Jesus.... You were born.... What? ... Emanuel.... The Most High God ... Jesus Christ.... Jehovah.... Oh, I like that."

Could Jesus have been showing Jessica the Lamb's Book of Life as she said, "Book? ... Me? ... It is? ... Today?" She let out a contented giggle and asked, "What number?"

Next, the Lord taught Jessica about the creation. She asked, "What about him? ... Adam? ... Eve? ... They were where? ... And the trees ... just everything but that one? ... That tree.... There was a snake? ... NO! That's the devil, that's right, huh? ... And what? ... She did it.... No, she took a bite and gave it to Adam and he didn't have to take a bite but he did, right? … And it was just as much his fault cause you told him…. Oh, you could have kept her from doing it…. But you must have wanted some too…. No?"

"Okay, you show me…. In the beginning was the Word and the Word was God…. Seven? … Everything? … Dominion over everything? … Animals, the birds? What? … You mean I don't have to worry? … You'll take care of me just like the sparrow…. Okay, I believe you."

After another long pause, Jessica sighed, "Yeah, you're all right," then paused again for another minute.

Jessica continued, "What? … One will be in … what? Two will be in the field, one will go and one will stay…. Why can't they both go? … Oh, because one's not ready. I'm ready. You take me … I'm going…. Will I be alive or dead when you come? … You can't answer that? … Okay."

"I love you more than anything in the whole world. And you know why? You probably already know. Just 'cause you sent somebody to me and I didn't even know it. What did you go to all that trouble for? … Because you love me? … And you wanted to teach them a lesson … Patience, and faith, and prayer, endurance, trust."

At this point, Jessica talked to the Lord for a while concerning Paul Dana, Grady, Pat, and me. The things she said indicated she was speaking with someone who knew us intimately. How I would have loved to have heard the Lord's words to Jessica at that point, but whatever he said to her will have to remain a mystery.

Jessica also mentioned our three year old son, Jeromy, and his healing from a condition he had had at birth. To me, this was one of the most astounding things of all. Jeromy had been born when we were living in Pennsylvania and Pat and I had not talked about his birth for almost three years.

The conversation switched back to the subject of Jesus' second coming. "You went to prepare a place for me? And you're coming back! Keep my lamp burning? Don't hide it under the bed? I won't. Don't want to start no fires."

"No man knoweth the day or the hour or the week or the month or nothing. But it's soon, huh?"

"I don't? That's good. Don't want to give up everything at once, you know. You'll tell me when it's time to quit smoking? Okay. Take your time. Already gave up drugs. I don't drink."

Another long pause followed before Jessica spoke again. "The thoughts and the dreams? I renounce the thoughts and the dreams in the name of the Lord Jesus Christ. I command them with the authority of the Lord Jesus Christ that they can't bother me any more. And I wash my mind in the blood of the Lord Jesus Christ and I challenge any demon that cometh forth. Thank you, Jesus."

From this point, Jessica talked some more about personal things including her family and friends. She became less coherent and the pauses grew longer. She sounded sleepy as she purred contentedly and a smile graced her face. We heard her voice intimate expressions of love to Jesus. "Yeah … huh? … You're warm…. I'm gonna like here…. I like your love. It's like no other love…. Ummmm, oh yeah."

Her last words in this incredible conversation with the Lord were: "You want me to do what? Read Psalm forty-two? Okay. You're talking about how the deer runs across the waters. That's the way we're supposed to long for you? Okay."

Jessica sighed and stirred, but was quiet for several minutes. Finally, she opened her eyes, stretched, and smiled as she said, "Wow, it sure does look different down here."

9

The Road Back to Reality

○ ○

But grow in grace, and in the knowledge of our Lord and Saviour Jesus Christ. To him be glory both now and for ever. Amen.

—*2 Peter 3:18*

Do not mock the Gospels and say there is no Satan. Evil is too real in the world to say that. Do not say the idea of Satan is dead and gone. Satan never gains so many cohorts, as when, in his shrewdness, he spreads the rumor that he is long since dead. Do not reject the Gospel because it says the Saviour was tempted. Satan always tempts the pure—the others are already his.

—*Fulton J. Sheen (1895–1979)*
Catholic Bishop and Apologist

Jessica stayed at our home in Augusta for a few more days following her deliverance. Her disposition was sweet and gentle and we never had another episode of demonic manifestations.

After Jessica's incredible experience of talking with the Lord, I was tempted to put her on some kind of spiritual pedestal. After all, I had been a born-again Christian for almost thirty years and Jesus had never talked to me like that. However, it didn't take long for us to realize who Jessica really was—an infant in Jesus Christ.

Others were also impressed as the news of Jessica's deliverance spread quickly throughout our church family and also the larger Augusta community. Several people called and asked if they could meet with Jessica. Some wanted to seek counsel from her because either they or someone they knew wanted to be set free from some bondage caused by involvement in the occult. They thought an ex-witch would be just the person to help them. One woman who led a Charismatic women's prayer and Bible study group wanted Jessica to speak at one of their meetings, to share her testimony. I told these people that Jessica was just a baby in Christ who still had much maturing to do as a Christian before she started ministering to others.

An evangelist came to see me at my office and asked if I would turn Jessica over to him. He said he specialized in ministering to the demon possessed and dealt with these kinds of things every day. I dismissed him as an opportunist who wanted to exploit Jessica for his own benefit.

Jessica attended church services with us on a few occasions and our church members were cordial and welcoming to her, but she was never publicly introduced or pointed out in church.

During the time Jessica stayed in our home, I had opportunity to question her closely about her experience. Although she remembered the gist of her conversation with the Lord on the night of her final deliverance, she could not recall all the details. She could not quote any of the scriptures which we had heard her repeating in the vision. Perhaps God had planted these things deep inside her heart and would bring them to her remembrance when she needed them. Or, maybe the vision had been as much for the benefit of those of us who ministered to her as it was for Jessica.

Jessica showed every evidence of being a genuinely reborn person. On Monday, Pat took her shopping for a new Bible to replace the used one I had given her. She also bought some jewelry with Christian symbols to replace that which represented her old life of witchcraft. That evening we took her to a bridge over the Savannah River and she voluntarily threw her silver skull ring into the water.

Jessica's appetite for the word of God was very keen and she spent hours reading her Bible. It was so refreshing to be able to answer her many innocent, childlike questions about the things she read.

On the second night after her deliverance, Jessica was alone in her room when she read Acts 19. This is the passage which tells of those who repented from practicing sorcery, gathered their occult books together, and burned them.

Conviction fell upon Jessica; she had a very restless night. Early the next morning, she informed me she needed to return to Savannah that very day to get rid of the three hundred books she had on witchcraft. She also wanted to pick up some of her clothing and personal items to bring back to Augusta with her.

I felt protective toward Jessica and would rather have kept her with us until she became more grounded in her newfound faith. I was concerned that if she returned to her witch friends, they would try to draw her back into her old ways. She reminded me that she already had a bus ticket to Savannah which I had given her and I had promised she could return whenever she wanted to do so.

I reasoned that if the Lord had been able to watch over Jessica and lead her to me the first time, then surely he would protect her from harm now that she was his child. Actually, I needed a rest myself. It had been more than a week since I had had a full night's sleep. Physically and emotionally, I was wrung out. I took Jessica to the bus station, bought her a return ticket to Augusta, and with a prayer for God's watchcare over her, I let her go.

From the beginning, I had suspected that Jessica might have been using an alias. The demon voices that had spoken through her had reinforced my suspicions. While Jessica was away, I did some investigating through contacts I had in Savannah. I learned Jessica's real name and a little more about her. In our first encounter at the Savannah hotel, Jessica had said several things about her ancestry, claiming that she came from a very prominent family of witches. This was not true.

Jessica was indeed a witch of high standing in a Savannah coven, but she was not related to Sybil Leek or Anton LaVey—except in a mystical sense. The things she had told me about her past would have led me to believe she was a very big witch. But, she was just an ordinary witch after all. Deception and vanity have been two of the hallmarks of Satan since his fall from Heaven. Jessica had displayed both traits.

During her two days back in Savannah, Jessica called me three times to ask for prayer. She lived with her mother and her stepfather. When Jessica told them about giving her heart to Jesus, the stepfather had slapped her and Jessica's mother had just turned away. Jessica said her stepfather later apologized for slapping her and tried to get her to go to bed with him. She almost did, because she desperately longed for love and acceptance. However, she managed to resist the temptation.

On the first night Jessica was home, some of her old friends came over to her house and tried to dissuade her away from her newfound Christian faith. Jessica left her friends sitting in the living room and went to an upstairs phone. She called and asked me to pray for her. As we talked, I heard someone begin to yell in the background. The yelling turned to rants and raves and Jessica shouted back, "Jesus loves you, Barney!"

I began to pray with Jessica over the telephone, with Barney still bellowing and cursing in the background. His rants and raves turned to growls—then a loud scream—and after that, all was quiet for a moment.

Jessica held the phone away, let out a loud whistle, and shouted down the stairs, "Hey you guys, something's wrong with Barney. He's passed out and is lying in the floor."

A thump indicated Jessica had laid down the phone. I heard nothing for two or three minutes except muffled voices and a few background noises. Then, Barney's voice could be heard again, sounding far away, "How did I get down here?"

Finally, Jessica picked the telephone back up and asked if I was still there. I told her I was listening. "Barney says he's got to leave," Jessica said. "Jeff is still here. I'll try to get away and call you back."

About two hours later, Jessica called again. She assured me everything was all right and asked if I would like to hear a poem she had written earlier that day. I said "Sure." As she read slowly, I jotted these words:

> Leading by a hand of kindness,
> Leading by a heart of care,
> Every moment I am leading,
> Though you may be unaware.
>
> Truly I'm a mighty Saviour,
> Faithful always to the task,
> Surely now my victory's sounding,
> And my blessings you can ask.
>
> Put your hand in mine and follow,
> Let obedience rule your mind,
> Humbling self in service meekly,
> That my purpose you may find.

I asked Jessica where she had gotten the poem. She said God just put the words in her mind.

The next day, Jessica called with good news. She reported that Barney had given his heart to Jesus. Also, she was making plans to return to Augusta the following morning and wanted to spend a couple of weeks with us. However, she was worried because her mom was having some of her witch friends over again that night and she feared that if any evil spirits should manifest themselves, they might harm her. I had already prepped Jessica carefully as to how she should respond in such an eventuality. "Remember, Jessica," I asked, "what will you do?"

Without hesitation she responded, "I will point my finger at them and say, I rebuke you in the name of the Lord Jesus Christ and I plead the power of his blood over you."

After making arrangements to pick Jessica up the next morning at the Augusta Greyhound terminal, I prayed with her again before we hung up. She arrived the next day, on schedule, and with a big smile on her face.

It troubled me that, once Jessica gave her heart to Jesus and was delivered from the demons, she had not come clean about her past. Upon her return to Augusta, I decided to confront her with the things I had learned about her.

On the first evening that Jessica was back in our home, Pat and I invited Paul Dana and his wife, Julie, over for a visit. The four of us told Jessica straightforward that we knew her real name and, in fact, had learned quite a bit about who she was. We did not know what kind of reaction to expect.

She began to cry. Jessica said she had wanted to tell us the truth, but was afraid that if we found out she was not really from a famous family of witches, we would no longer love her.

Another suspicion of mine was also confirmed. Jessica admitted that she had never called me from either Atlanta or Aiken, but had been in Savannah all the time. The intriguing thing about this was the uncannily accurate description she had given us of the telephone booth on the side of the road near Aiken.

Jessica said she had used astro-projection. By this means, she would meditate about a certain place until in her mind, she was actually there. She also said that in the past she had sometimes become confused and had a hard time deciphering fantasy from reality.

We assured Jessica that we loved her for who she was. Now that she was a child of God, she was our sister. This opened the door for two fruitful weeks in which we were able to teach Jessica much about our Lord.

For three days during that time, Pat, our boys, and I took Jessica camping at Hunting Island State Park on the South Carolina coast. The boys had a spring break from school and this gave us an unusual opportunity to be with Jessica away from the distractions of the everyday business of the church.

One day on the beach I noticed that Jessica seemed despondent. When I asked her why, she confessed that she missed her psychic powers. She had become bored lying in the sun and had tried to use astro-projection to escape in her mind. She had traveled frequently in this manner for many years, but now it wouldn't work for her any more.

Jessica's visit to our home was one of her first exposures to normal Christian family life. Her father had deserted her and her mother when Jessica was still an infant. Jessica could not remember her real dad, but she had been told that he was into witchcraft. She had no way of knowing for sure.

Jessica had never communicated much with her mother, although her mother also dabbled in the occult. As a child, she spent many long hours playing by herself in her room. While she was still very young, playing alone one afternoon, she said she saw a little creature sitting in the corner of her room watching her. She ran to tell her mother, who said that she was imagining things and the little creature did not exist.

Jessica never bothered her mother again but accepted the creature, and others who later appeared, as her playmates. She said these playmates taught her many things, but she never was sure if they were for real or just make believe. Gradually, as she grew older, the playmates stopped appearing to her.

Jessica developed a great interest in the occult and began to read everything she could on the subject from books she found at the Savannah Public Library. It amazed her when she read things which her playmates had taught her many years before.

For example, in one of the books she saw a drawing of a pentagram. One of the little playmates had taught her to draw a pentagram and had told her of its magical significance. She had never really believed the playmates until she saw the things they had taught her confirmed in the books from the library.

Experiences like these were enough to convince Jessica that witchcraft was real. Since her mother had given her no spiritual training, witchcraft became her religion.

At the age of thirteen, Jessica located a coven of witches in Savannah and began attending their meetings. She dropped out of school to devote all of her time to the pursuit of the Witch's Craft.

By the age of fifteen, she had already engaged in her first human sacrifice. It was of a newborn infant which had been born in a commune for the sole purpose of being ritualistically offered to Satan. Jessica became a full-fledged witch and within a few years achieved enough stature in the craft that she sometimes traveled to covens in various parts of the country to give talks on mysticism.

There had been plenty of ups and downs in Jessica's career as a witch. Two or three times earlier she had made an effort to investigate Christianity.

After first becoming a witch, Jessica had regularly attended a Catholic church. She was not a Catholic, but was there on assignment to steal holy water and communion wafers which were desecrated and used in witchcraft ceremonies.

When she was nineteen, Jessica had contacted a Baptist pastor in an effort to break a drug habit that she could no longer handle. She lived with a Christian family and attended the Baptist church for several months. However, she told me, during that time she never heard a sermon. It was as though her mind went into a state of suspension whenever the Bible was read or the minister began to preach. She said she went forward in this church once just to get people off her back. All the while, she was still secretly practicing her witchcraft late at night after the family was asleep.

Once she had visited a Pentecostal church. About halfway through the service, a sense of panic came over her. She jumped up, bolted for the exit, and in her haste, ran into the front door so hard that she cracked it. It happens that I was a friend of the pastor of the church in Savannah where Jessica said this took place. I later called the pastor. He said he remembered the incident, but he did not know who Jessica was and never saw her again.

About six months before she contacted me, Jessica had decided to visit another church near where she lived. Upon entering the lobby one Sunday morning, she was accosted by an usher who quickly informed her that ladies were not allowed into that church wearing blue jeans. He told her to go home, put on a dress, and come back. At the time, the only skirts Jessica owned were her spring and fall ceremonial witch's robes. She never returned to that church.

Even with her miraculous deliverance, Jessica still had some very deep emotional scars which needed healing. During the few years I kept in contact with her, I saw Jessica make remarkable progress in her Christian walk. She disassociated herself from old friends and began attending a Full-Gospel church that I helped her find. There she found a home fellowship group which she said took her in "just like I'm family." As she continued in the Word, in prayer, in worship, and in fellowship, I saw her blossoming into the beautiful woman of God that she was created to be.

Epilogue

After Jessica's deliverance, she went back to using her real name. However, I have continued to call her Jessica in this book to protect her privacy. I kept in touch with Jessica for about five years after our first encounter. During that time, she never returned to witchcraft and continued in her Christian faith—happy and free in Jesus. Unfortunately, I have lost touch with Jessica over the years. My hope is that she, or someone who knows her, might read this book and contact me.

Paul Dana Walker, my youth minister who played such a remarkable role in Jessica's deliverance, was one of the most gifted young ministers I have ever known. In all of my 35 years as a senior pastor, I have never had a staff member who was more effective, more dedicated, or more loyal. He was also one of my closest friends.

Tragically, Paul Dana was killed on November 19, 1980, at the age of twenty four. He died in a head-on collision on Interstate-20 near Atlanta about eight months after Jessica's deliverance. Paul Dana's beautiful wife, Julie, miraculously survived the crash which was caused by a drunk driver going the wrong way down the Interstate. However, Julie had severe multiple injuries which took many months to heal. The following Spring Paul Dana was scheduled to graduate from

Augusta College (now Augusta State University) with his master's degree in psychology. The school awarded the degree to him posthumously and his widow, Julie, walked the aisle to receive the degree in his memory. Paul Dana was already making plans to enter a Ph.D. program at the University of Tennessee. Now all of his dreams, plans, and potential would never be realized.

Paul Dana's death made no sense at all to me. My only consolation was the faith that our omniscient God, the giver and taker of life, sees things from an eternal perspective which is beyond my temporal comprehension. Still I wondered, why would God take such a gifted and promising young man home at such an early age?

I was one of four ministers to speak at Paul Dana's funeral which was held at the Mount Paran Church of God in Atlanta, a mega-church pastored by his father, Dr. Paul L. Walker. At the funeral, I read from I Corinthians 13:12: *"For now we see through a glass darkly, but then face to face: now I know in part; but then shall I know as even also I am known."*

I did not share my doubts with the congregation of more than 2,000 people who attended his funeral. Instead, I shared my faith. "Paul Dana now sees what we do not yet see; he now knows what we do not yet know; he now understands what we do not yet understand."

Paul Dana had been a star athlete while doing his undergraduate studies in Cleveland, Tennessee. The Paul Dana Walker Arena at Lee University, his alma mater, is named in Paul Dana's honor.

Julie recovered from her injuries and returned for a while to Augusta, where she served as our church's Minister of Youth. Julie later remarried and today she is a highly successful leadership speaker and trainer.

Grady Mosley (H. Grady Mosley, II) later answered the call of God to preach. He was married in 1983 and received his Masters of Divinity degree from Candler School of Theology at Emory University in 1985. Today, he serves as a senior pastor in the North Georgia Conference of the United Methodist Church. God has blessed Grady and his wife, Deborah, with three children, including a son named Paul Dana. Grady says his greatest passion is "preaching and sharing the good news of Jesus Christ."

I remained as pastor of the church in Augusta for twelve more years, until 1992. I then moved on to other assignments, serving as pastor of churches in Georgia, North Carolina and Tennessee. Today, I continue in ministry, but am retired from the pastorate.

With this small volume, I add to the many books which others have already written about demonic possession. The testimony of Jessica's deliverance fills a void in that it may be one of the most comprehensive narrative of an exorcism ever published in a Protestant, Evangelical context. I offer it as a straightforward and honest account of a life-changing adventure of faith in which God allowed me to witness his supernatural power triumphing over the forces of Satan. May God use it for His Glory!